Only

D0293491

Only Connect

Worship and Liturgy from the Perspective of Pastoral Care

ROBIN GREEN

Foreword by H. A. Williams

Darton, Longman and Todd
London

First published in 1987 by
Darton, Longman and Todd Ltd
89 Lillie Road, London SW6 1UD

Reprinted 1988

© 1987 Robin Green

ISBN 0 232 51719 3

British Library Cataloguing in Publication Data

Green, Robin
  Only connect: worship and liturgy from the
perspective of pastoral care.
  1. Pastoral psychology
  I. Title
  253.5   BV4012

ISBN 0–232–51719–3

Phototypeset by Input Typesetting Ltd, SW19 8DR
Printed and bound by Anchor Brendon Ltd
Tiptree, Essex

Contents

Foreword

It is more important for a writer to ask questions than to prescribe answers, because the only answers which have for us the power of truth are those we discover for ourselves. That does not mean that it is useless for a writer to give hints towards possible answers, for these may spark off within us the activity of searching and, maybe, finding. The writer's crucial task is to kindle within his readers the creative power of his own search. And this search, if it is to lead to anything of value, must be undertaken by everything we are, by our feelings and actions no less than by our thinking.

The tremendous importance of Robin Green's book lies, I believe, in its posing of fundamental questions about the meaning and practice of the Christian gospel which disturb the assumptions and preconceptions we are generally unaware of holding, particularly when we are engaged in communal worship. He will not allow us to bypass our need to discover how we can connect what we do in church with the various levels of our human experience, especially that part of it which is painful and destructive.

The fact that the answers he suggests are no more than elusive hints which leave the reader unsatisfied and wanting to ask further questions is one of the book's greatest merits. Robin Green does not pretend to do for us what we can do only for ourselves. So, for instance, he insists upon our imperative need 'of a renewed vision of those great symbols which are latent in every person and which are celebrated in the cosmic and metaphysical dramas of humanity'. He does indeed provide examples of those symbols. Taken, as they are, from contemporary life they will speak powerfully to many. But in the end Robin Green leaves it to the reader to find out how and in what form this or the other symbol is alive for him or herself.

Robin Green is at his most courageous when he raises the problem of the connection of prayer and worship with the shadow side of our nature, what in a striking image he calls the stinking darkness which is part of each of us.

Christian writers have often spoken of our humanity being taken up into God. What in fact they have meant is the repression in the subconscious of a great deal of what we are so that only half of us – the respectable pious half – is offered to God to make his own, while the stinking darkness is left to itself to fester unseen and work its evil spell upon us disguised in this or the other religiously acceptable form.

Robin Green will have none of this. He argues that since the stinking darkness is a real and valid component of our selfhood, then a way must be found of including it in both our individual and communal response to God. For only so can that response be genuinely wholehearted. Worship, he says, is the place where by means of symbols the conscious and unconscious confront each other so that what we offer in our liturgies can be really and fully ourselves.

He does not claim adequately to have solved the problem of how we can do this. But he points us in valuable directions. And his emphasis on the urgent necessity of our discovering how in worship we can connect our generally unacknowledged shadow side with the self we do acknowledge, supplies what I believe to be the challenge most desperately needed in Christian life today. For we are much more acutely aware than past ages that it is precisely by loving and cherishing the Beast that he becomes the Prince Charming he really is – a transformation which is the greatest of God's miracles.

Robin Green's book can thus be called revolutionary. Revolutions do not offer security, still less comfort, to the complacent. If we take Robin Green's book seriously, even the most devout among us, perhaps especially the devout, will be more than a little disturbed. But it will be the sort of disturbance which leads to new life as we are shaken out of the cosy grave of our spiritual habits. What we took for granted as the objective reality solidly there will be recognized, in part at least, as no more than the effect of the distorting spectacles through which we are looking. It is no mean achievement to have thus cleansed the doors of perception. And which of us can claim that we have no need of such cleansing? That is what makes this book a must for all who accept the Christian gospel as the mainspring of their lives.

H. A. WILLIAMS

Thanksgiving

My life has been enriched and supported by numerous people; so there is a sense in which they are all part of this book. But there are some to whom I owe an enormous debt of gratitude.

I am deeply indebted to my friends and colleagues in the International Association of Pastoral Care and Counselling who have sown all kinds of seeds for me and have encouraged me to make this exploration.

My team colleagues in the Diocese of Southwark lay-training team gave me a lot of space to write this book.

Jean Wadsworth did a great deal of the editing and Lesley Riddle and Victoria Le Fanu completed the process. Dr David Tripp of Lincoln Theological College confirmed for me that there is a theology for the imagination and offered me more food for thought.

Tris Lipscombe and Francisco de Francesca struggled with countless versions of the manuscript.

My daughters, Ruth and Kirsten, are a constant reminder to me of the need to go on envisioning the future against all the threats to our humanity.

Then I owe a great debt to my closest friends and especially to Graham. He supported me through some very dark days as I completed this book. Those who have loved me have given me the courage to live against the darkness.

Finally I must thank God for the gift of living at the frontiers and in places where I could make the connections. It's a hell of a place to be, but I don't want to be anywhere else. It's made a priest of me.

London   ROBIN GREEN
September 1986

I kiss my hand
  to the stars, lovely-asunder
Starlight, wafting him out of it; and
  Glow, glory in thunder.
Kiss my hand to the dappled with damson west:
Since, tho' he is under the world's splendour and wonder,
  His mystery must be instressed, Stressed;
For I greet him the days I meet him,
  And bless when I understand.

GERALD MANLEY HOPKINS
'The Wreck of the Deutschland'

Prologue

I was walking through Southwark in London towards the
river Thames. It was a desolate wasteland covered with heaps
of rubble and debris. Between the decayed boulders twisted
the wizened stems of plane trees, grey with the dust of time.
I walked in the direction of Southwark Cathedral. It still
stood, blackened against the grey London sky. What had once
stood immersed in the hubbub of working life, now stood
dark and lifeless in this dust-laden landscape.

I reached the door of the cathedral. It stood locked and
barred. A momentary flash of terror froze me to the spot.
This was the place where vocation had been sanctified with
meaning. I wandered round the dark walls until I found a
tiny door I had not expected. It stood ajar. But to get inside
you had to bend very low.

The interior of the building was suffused with a pale golden
light. It had the warmth and depth of well worn gold. It
illuminated the faces of children, alive with laughter, sitting
in a great circle in the centre of the cathedral. In the circle
clowns tumbled and gyrated in every direction. I went and
sat with the children. They laughed at my painted nose.

Then from the tiny door came a piercing yell: 'Why is the
land burnt and nobody passes by?'

I have been fascinated for over twenty years by the connections between worship and human need. What does it mean
for people to be drawn close to the love of God in worship?
What is going on inside people as they worship God? What
is happening as people engage in the Church's liturgy? I have
become increasingly convinced that pastoral insights, as much
as new developments in liturgical reform, could contribute to

the renewal of the Church's worship. It seemed possible that
these insights might also increase the confidence of those who
have the responsibility of leading worship.

I am sure that this concern began with the dream which I
have just recounted. My thinking has been profoundly
influenced by C. G. Jung, with two aspects of his thought
having especial significance:

(a) Worship develops a proper sense of worth and value both
in relation to God and to ourselves. Carl Jung's exploration
of archetypes and the human psyche has had a particularly
important bearing on my thinking.

(b) The impulse to worship springs in the first instance from
the human unconscious. We have, therefore, to struggle with
the whole of our human experience as we worship God. Jung's
exploration of the human shadow and human light is an
indicator of the depth of human experience a book like this
must struggle with. If worship is about the whole self
responding to God, then some very difficult human questions
must be faced and addressed. Jung's further study of the
process of 'individuation' offered me more clues in this area.

There was another sense in which it was no accident that
the beginning of my thinking was a dream. As we explore
together the relationship between pastoral care and worship,
we shall meet the human need both to order experience and
to express the encounter with God in non-verbal languages.
At many times in the writing of this book I have longed for
the skill to draw pictures and make music: language wasn't
adequate to express what I was thinking and feeling. In his
play, *Equus*, Peter Shaffer touches on this connection:
'Without worship, you shrink: it's as brutal as that.' The
word-play around 'shrink', a slang word for psychiatrist,
underlines the relationship between how we understand
ourselves and the worship of God. Peter Shaffer's exploration
raises questions about how human personality is fulfilled
beyond itself, especially when we are faced with uncontrol-
lable forces. The choice may well be, as Teilhard de Chardin
suggested, between suicide and adoration.

The central argument of this book is, therefore, that
worship and liturgy care for us. God, through them, pays
loving attention to us and we in turn are able to express the
whole of our human experience to God. Worship is able by

its very nature to touch some of the deepest springs of the human psyche and to help us to face those sides of our self that we dare not face. Pastoral insights are able to help us understand the complex needs and hopes that we bring to worship. Without them, I believe there is a real risk that liturgy will become increasingly archaic and sterile. But if we can connect our worship and our pastoral care many fruitful areas of renewal and change will be opened up.

This book is therefore an invitation to others to explore and to go on opening up new lines of inquiry and areas of thought. I know of only two other books which have attempted to make the connections. One is published in the U.S.A., the other in Germany. But it is clear that the field is one which engages the imagination and concern of many people in many traditions, Christian and Jewish. Although I write out of an Anglican context, I believe that what I have to say is of direct relevance to people in all these traditions. At an international conference in Finland in 1985, I ran a two-day workshop on the topic. The workshop engaged the interest and insights of people from many different cultures and was one of the biggest workshops at the conference. People are beginning to make the connections between worship and pastoral care all over the world. This book is an offering towards that exploration: an invitation to 'only connect'.

1

The Landscape of Love

But I doubt whether even the most fervent moderniser could believe that if only the choir had been singing rock and roll, if only the lessons had proclaimed God the True Integration of Self, then the whole nave would have been full with cheerful and loud-voiced participants, greatly to the detriment of the takings that afternoon by Peterborough United Football Club. (PHILIP TOYNBEE)

Soon after arriving in his first parish a young priest, Tom, was invited by the warden of an old people's home to celebrate a monthly Eucharist in the home. He agreed to do so. He arrived on the appointed day, set up an altar, handed out copies of the Alternative Service Book, Rite A Eucharist, and invited the people present to choose some hymns. The voices piped up: 'Abide with me', 'The Old Rugged Cross', 'The Day Thou Gavest . . . ' 'Oh,' said Tom, 'they all seem a bit grim.' He began to celebrate the Eucharist.

When the time for communion came only two people out of the twenty-two present received the bread and wine. Tom was puzzled.

After the Eucharist was over he sat talking with some of the elderly people. His puzzlement had grown so he asked gently why so few had wanted to receive communion. One old lady sat staring at him with silent, hostile eyes. Another said: 'Can't stand that new-fangled Lord's Prayer.' Others seemed to nod consent. Then there was a long pause. A man sitting nearby interrupted the uneasy silence: 'We're not worth it . . . "Ye that do truly and earnestly repent of your sins". . . .' Then he stopped and stared bleakly in front of him.

Tom was still puzzled and during the next week reflected on the experience. He decided to ring up the warden and ask

about the history of the Eucharist. She told him that until a
few months ago it had been taken by a Free Church pastor.
Then she added: 'Poor loves, he did nothing but harangue
them about their sins. As you can imagine, they've got plenty
of chances to break the Ten Commandments in here!'

The next monthly visit came round. Tom went armed with
copies of the Book of Common Prayer! But before starting
the Eucharist he sat down and explored with the group the
picture of Jesus sitting down and sharing a meal with a rag
bag of humanity. He talked of real humility, knowing that
you are hungry and need food and being ready to receive. He
talked of the value each person has and how the grace of God
enhances that sense of personal worth.

When the time for communion came, everyone present
received the bread and the wine.

Worship cares for us. Inappropriate liturgy can strip us of
our sense of worth and dignity. This case-study raises some
basic issues about the relationship of worship and pastoral
care. These include the importance of continuity and familiarity; the appropriateness of different liturgies for different
groups; the relationship of image and symbol to human needs;
the ways in which the proclamation of the Word of God
connects with actual human experience. Perhaps most
importantly the incident raises a question which is frequently
ignored in liturgical debate; 'What does God want from us
in worship?' Tom was faced with that question. He also had
some understanding of the psychological make-up of human
beings. Out of the perplexing questions grew both imaginative
pastoral care and more satisfying liturgy. The pastoral insight
also made him less anxious about using new liturgical rites.
Theological-college enthusiasm gave way to real pastoral
need.

The popular image of pastoral care is a meeting between
two people relying heavily on individual skills derived from
psycho-therapeutic models. The aim of the care is self-fulfil-
ment and self-help. That is the model that many people
have of pastoral care, and models are very influential. This
particular one has been powerfully influenced by the American thinker, Carl Rogers, whose counselling methods

continue to influence pastoral care and counselling training
in this country. It may be a radical shift, therefore, to think
about liturgy as a model of pastoral care, so it is important
to explore the differences and some of the underlying philosophical assumptions.

One of the key developments in the history of pastoral care
in the twentieth century was the adoption of a medical model
based on a methodological relationship between pastoral care
and psychology. In the U.S.A., and much more recently in
Britain, part of the formation for priesthood and for other
kinds of professional ministry has been focused on a model
of clinical pastoral education in which ordinands and others
have reflected on 'the living human documents', i.e. people
in crisis. A hospital or prison or psychiatric clinic becomes a
laboratory for self-discovery, and the models are often doctors,
psychiatric social workers, hospital chaplains engaged in
team-work with individual patients. The student begins to
discover something about the elements of psychodynamic
theory, counselling techniques and individual pastoral care.
There is little doubt that where students have been committed
to such an experience, it has influenced their personal growth
and pastoral relationships. I can vouch personally for the
truth of that. Nevertheless if we analyse it within its own
terms of reference it does have some serious limitations.

First of all it is possible for some priests to make counselling
the chief function of ministry at the expense of other essential
tasks. Nowhere is this more clearly highlighted than in the
preparation and conduct of worship as 'the work of the people
of God'. For the majority of clergy there is always a risk that
they will understand their identity through one particular
model. Other elements within ministry will either be taken
for granted or simply tackled as routine tasks. That seems
like a recipe for a growing lack of integrity. It will certainly
make for frustration within the minister. It is equally true
that when clergy develop a liturgical lust at the expense
of pastoral care, aridity and ecclesiastical myopia quickly
develop.

My second question relates to the philosophical basis of
some pastoral care models. If there are theological questions
about some models of pastoral care, we have to be cautious
about relating those models to the area of worship and liturgy.

In a period, in which Auschwitz, Hiroshima and the Gulag Archipelago have dominated the human imagination, it is hardly surprising that the reconstruction of the notion of personal responsibility has developed. This kind of torment demanded a new response:

> Then she started to understand that the sound came from the mass of people moving slightly as they settled down and were pressed tighter by the movements of the ones who were still living.
>
> She had fallen into a bath of blood. She lay on her right side, and her right arm lay under her, at an unnatural angle. It did not hurt. She could not move or turn, because something else, presumably another body, was trapping her right hand. She felt no pain anywhere. Apart from the rustling there were other strange subterranean sounds, a dull chorus of groaning, choking and sobbing. She tried to call her son's name, but no voice would come. (D. M. Thomas)[1]

Existentialism has provided part of the response to the mass suffering and courage of our collective history. In its stress on the possibility of self-knowledge and the human capacity for self-analysis it has provided a basis for some of the major counselling theories. Carl Rogers suggests that nothing is to be done which would compromise the freedom of another person. Counselling is to be client-centred and value judgements are to be avoided. Above all else the individual is to be given ultimate significance.

Existentialism does provide a compelling vision. Because it endows individuals with a sense of their personal worth, it militates against dehumanisation, the seedbed of nuclear warfare. It also puts another person struggling to take responsibility for their own life at the centre of our concern. But there is a paradox in existentialism. It describes what it means for people to stand against all that threatens their existence. But it does not take account of people as social beings. It highlights the centrality of individuality and uniqueness. But it doesn't really enter into the struggle of understanding the rhythm between uniqueness and community. I shall argue later in this chapter that that is part of the struggle within liturgy. Pastoral insights based on the existentialist vision cannot be applied simply to worship and liturgy. Nevertheless that same vision is a reminder that liturgy cannot be regarded as another mass movement. It alerts us to the needs of the individual within any corporate action.

If the existentialist basis of some pastoral care is not an adequate basis for understanding the needs of those who engage in worship, we must find a more adequate basis. This is a practical need because, like the young priest at the beginning of the chapter, we may have visions about how people are, which prove inadequate when faced with the complexity of their needs in worship. There is a proper Christian existentialism, which will celebrate the unique pilgrimage of every individual into God. When that sense of uniqueness is lost, women and men are caged in categories, and stereotypes and caricatures start. It would have been only too easy for Tom to have gone on with a caricature of 'old people'.

The Christian understanding of a person is based on a view of human personality as sacramental. There is an essential mystery about every human being because there are aspects of each of us about which we shall never know all that there is to know. There is something infinite which gives to people an inalienable dignity. The Christian believes that human life, however paralysed, however dark, however compromised, perverted, marginalised or smashed up, has been taken up into the life of God. It cannot be judged on its own terms alone. The claim that human life is not only mysterious but perverted in its true purpose has to be assessed on the basis of all the facts available to us. But if people sense an inward mystery, does that not help us understand why some people look to worship as a source of care? Worship cares for people because at some level we sense that we are made 'in the image of God'. That dimension of mystery also challenges some of the subtly omnipotent fantasies which afflict those who are in the business of caring for others.

With that understanding of the mysterious dimensions of human personality we can shift to a different way of seeing worship. *Liturgy, which is the vehicle through which worship is expressed, creates an environment in which human beings confront those sides of themselves which under normal circumstances they dare not face.* This revised view of human personality challenges some of the assumptions that pastoral counsellors sometimes make. Nevertheless there is an increasing awareness among counsellors that those assumptions require further examination. You cannot care for another person without some reference to values and ultimately to what you believe the destiny of human life is. Those who exercise a ministry of pastoral care and counselling within a Christian context believe that Jesus is the paradigm for understanding what the final status of human life is. He is a moment of disclosure in whom we see human life in a new way. Christian pastoral care will always embody that claim to a greater or lesser degree. Pastoral care and liturgy come remarkably close to fulfilling the same function. Both offer ways of seeing ourselves and God.

My third area of difficulty about the normal models of pastoral care is this. They under-rate the social dimensions of human personality and so develop a tendency to divorce pastoral care from social and political concerns. But there are always questions to be asked about why more attention is not paid to the causes of human affliction. Marxism has provided one framework within which to understand the relationship of human well-being to socio-political and economic structures. The insights of Marxist thinking have inspired many radical attempts to stand alongside the poor in achieving a new economic order. But the actual operation of classical Marxism has failed to produce a credible understanding of the personal which would sustain a model of pastoral care.

This is central to our subject because, whatever else it is, worship is a corporate experience. The retreat into 'private lives' may be one of the most sinister developments of our time. It also threatens the development of worship and liturgy. Despite those threats people still experience worship as an environment in which the potential for community exists. I use the word 'potential' because I may be open to the charge that I am idealising liturgy and worship. I do not underestimate the incredible boredom, lack of imagination and suffocating ecclesiasticism that murders worship all over the world. I am convinced that the insights in this book will begin to renew liturgy because they address some of the root causes of that boredom. A good deal of liturgical reform only deals with the symptoms. By trying to face some of the causes, we might begin to release some of the potential that always exists in the encounter between God and people.

If worship is a corporate experience we need a corporate view of human personality to match that experience. Gerald Manley Hopkins has a telling phrase about human uniqueness: 'three numbered form'. It is the Christian claim that each human being can only be completed beyond her or himself. That completion comes both through the neighbour and through God. Human life is capable of being both uniquely itself and shared with the neighbour. Laurens van der Post, writing of his friendship with Carl Jung, said he had found 'a neighbour inside himself'. Jesus renamed his disciples 'friends':

> As we have affirmed more than once before, human misery stems ultimately from a three-fold alienation – alienation from God, alienation from our fellows, alienation from our own true being – of which the alienation from God is the root of the other two. Through Christ, we believe, God has acted to end this alienation by inviting us to be his friends. For only friendship with God ... can give us the inner security which makes it possible both to love our fellows and to live out our own truth.   (C. Bryant)[2]

I have tried to analyse in some detail my questions about some models of pastoral care and pastoral counselling because I hope that will help to remove some of the blocks to understanding how worship cares for us. But there is another problem. The individualistic nature of some Protestant liturgy also prevents it from mediating care. There is an uneasy correspondence between existentialism and Protestantism. The Reformation never produced a parallel revolution in pastoral care to that in theology, liturgy and doctrine. There is some evidence that new forms of pastoral care began, like Richard Baxter's systematic pastoral visitations. And at a later period the Wesleyan 'Classes' (House Groups) developed important links between care and worship. But in other significant ways a divorce happened between liturgy and care.

Pastoral care came to be understood as individual dealings

between the pastor and his 'flock', and many of the sacramental means of healing and grace fell into disuse. The practice of private confession and anointing were pre-eminent
among those. Exaggerated claims and abuses had existed in
the medieval church. The Reformers shifted to a lifestyle
which was almost exclusively cerebral. The iconoclasm of the
Commonwealth period accelerated that shift into an over-
verbal liturgy. This eventually sustained the idea of the 'portmanteau parson', a model still deeply influential in the
Anglican and Free-church traditions; all the gifts are in the
'portmanteau'. It eroded a proper sense of the Body of Christ
as a 'sustaining, healing, reconciling, guiding community'.[3]

That had its corresponding effect in worship and the
liturgy. The Reformers intended that worship should cease
being the exclusive domain of the clergy in order to become
the work of the people of God. Their efforts ended by virtually
dissolving the sacramental life, fragmenting corporate
worship into private devotion, heightening the role of the
clergyman over against the people of God and embracing a
highly individualistic gospel which too often left people
claiming, like the elderly man in our case study, 'We're not
worth it. . . .' The liturgy, which since the New Testament
had been the most important source of pastoral care, was
eroded into 'the flight of the alone to the Alone' (Plotinus).
Schleiermacher gave that its ultimate expression: 'The
mission of a priest in the world is a private business and the
temple should be a private chamber, where he lifts up his
voice to give utterance to religion.'

It is only very recently that the Protestant churches have
begun to restore liturgy to its status as 'the work of the people
of God'. They are beginning to recover something of the
New Testament experience of worship, which was a way of
understanding the whole of a Christian's experience of herself,
her neighbour and God! It was an environment of meaning:

The minister has a clear duty to counsel the ill and dying,
but he should first have helped create a community with a
religio-cultural view of the meaning of illness and death.
Certainly the minister should counsel persons with
marriage problems, sexual problems and divorce problems,
but he should first have helped to create among his people

a positive vision of the normative meaning of marriage, sexuality, and even divorce. The difficulty with much of pastoral counselling today is that more time is spent discussing the roots of counselling than in the more challenging process of developing the structure of meaning that should constitute the context for counselling.
(D. Browning)[4]

I want now to explore further the notion that liturgy is an *environment* within which people worship. I believe that the idea of environment is a helpful one because the ecology movement has reminded us that a good environment is a key to health. The delicate balances and counter-balances within organic life are a reminder that in all created order there is a proper interdependence. When any part of the ecology is destroyed, all other parts are affected. Hiroshima meant that the world could never be the same again because part of the world had been made sterile. This concept of environment applied to worship can help us to explore that dynamic interdependence, which is one of the clues to being human.

Liturgy provides people with an environment of *meaning*. It is the primary way in which the corporate faith of the church is communicated and appropriated. It is sometimes said that Methodists derive most of their doctrine from their hymns. Believing has become an individual affair under the impact of existentialism and the mass media. Instead of 'we believe', we hear 'my opinion is': radio phone-ins and television chat shows rarely reveal a deepening of insight. Instead we live in an age of analysis in which everything is dissected according to the participants of the programmes. The breaking through of new truth is a rare event. In one way that is liberating. It enhances a society where freedom of speech is a demonstrable reality. But there is another sense in which it leaves people confused and fragmented. It pushes people back on their own resources to make judgements, which they may not always have the capacity to do.

One important way in which liturgy functions as an environment of meaning is its capacity to contain corporate visions and to transmit social forms of believing. Those beliefs are the inherited traditions that mould the perceptions of certain groups of people: disclosures of what it means to be human at a rock-bottom level. Liturgy is able to bridge the gap between corporate ways of believing and the individual struggle to believe. If liturgy is an environment of meaning, it is a space in which people are 'sustained, guided, healed and reconciled'.

It is also a space to struggle with political and social issues. Dorothy Sayers explores this tension in her play *The Just Vengeance*:

> AIRMAN: No! No! No! What made me start off like that? I reacted automatically to the word 'creed' – My personal creed is something totally different.
>
> RECORDER: What is speaking in you is the voice of the city, The church and Household of Christ, your people and country
> From whom you derive. Did you think you were unbegotten? Unfranchised? With no community and no past?
> Out of the darkness of your unconscious memory
> The Stones of the city are crying out. Go on.[5]

That phrase 'the darkness of your unconscious memory' is a key to reflecting about worship and care. There is a desire within people, however inarticulate, to make sense of human experience. Liturgy, by providing a structure of meaning, helps us respond to that desire. It also creates a safe environment to push our questions hard and face perplexity. People come to church to be with God and to hide from God, to scream at God and to embrace God, to be with others and to be with themselves, to prepare for death and birth, marriage and divorce. Worship at its best is a place where people confront the depth of their own need in the presence of God. It can also be a place where people transcend the 'normal' relationships in their lives. I remember talking with the chaplain of a psychiatric hospital. He pointed out that the only time that 'we' was used in the hospital by staff and patients together was in the Christian Eucharist. For the rest of the time it was 'us' and 'them'.

I believe that this tension between corporate belief and human experience is far closer to the symbolic and concrete biblical traditions than the revival of ancient liturgical texts which characterises a lot of liturgical reform. The writers of liturgy have to find ways of developing non-coercive language in which we can explore how we perceive ourselves within the life of the community. The biblical tradition is far more plastic in its ways of appropriating the depths of human experience than most contemporary liturgical rites. (See also chapter 7 for the treatment of biblical language and sexism.) Liturgy may be conservative by nature but the reformers of it have much to learn from biblical criticism.

The believing community, expressing itself through an environment of meaning in liturgy and worship, is creating a zone of freedom in which individuals can face choices. Even when liturgy is turgid 'beyond belief' the tiniest glimmer of that still occurs. No liturgical action is complete unless it holds positive and negative elements at one. In fact no human being is complete until the opposites and polarities of human life live at harmony within that person. Worship offers a pattern of meanings, which begin to integrate experience. It offers a vision of where the resources might be discovered for our restoration in Christ as human beings. It also begins to make sense of the polarities within ourselves by offering a symbolic framework, which speaks to 'the darkness of our unconscious memory'.

Worship and liturgy can never be focussed solely around the pastoral needs of people. If it did, we should simply ask, 'What do we want from worship?' That sounds like a typical church council item or a session on a residential weekend run by the diocesan adult education officer! It suggests that we can be fulfilled within ourselves and that is a dangerous illusion. But if we can begin to see worship as a context for pastoral care, we shall then begin to envisage ways in which our self-understanding is enlarged by a dynamic under-standing of faith. Pastoral encounters frequently raise issues of ethical significance which cannot be resolved simply by an appeal to a value-free acceptance of personal responsibility. How do you pray at the bedside of a woman who has just had an abortion? How will you pray at the beginning of a church meeting if everyone knows that the married curate ran off with the churchwarden's daughter last week? Worship can care because it is capable of articulating those theological and ethical dimensions which otherwise might be difficult to express.

The story is told of a factory in the U.S.A. which at the time of the assassination of John Kennedy decided to hold a 'liturgy' to mark the event. Although the 'liturgy' was in no sense an orthodox Christian event, subsequent research revealed that the quality of working relationships in the factory was significantly better – both before and even more so afterwards – than in those taking part in the comparative study. I believe that this secular gathering offers a second clue to the way in which liturgy creates an environment. It creates an environment of *belonging*. Most hurt and pain, particularly emotional and psychological hurt, emerges in a social context, and especially in the family. It is important to recognise that belonging is likely to play an important role therefore in the healing and restorative process. Many anthropologists have written about the integrative effect of worship on groups of people. The common beliefs, as well as the common rituals and symbols, contribute to that integration. Integration, as Douglas Davies shows, is one of the foundation stones of a sense of belonging:

> . . . symbols can bring an individual to integrate disparate experiences of life. This is an important area for all concerned with people, their experiences and their thought . . . for myths enable an integration of thoughts and affectivity as they bring about an intuitional grasp of ideas and situations.[6]

Part of the genius of liturgy is its ability to hold in tension individual and corporate responses. As such it is an important form of preventative care. Two basic human fears are like flip sides of a coin. One of our deepest fears is that of being left completely alone. The other is the terror that my life will be taken over by another person so that I am stripped of my uniqueness. Many inner-city inhabitants have a versicle which says: 'We keep ourselves to ourselves'. The Christian doctrine of the Trinity is deeply influential in the symbolism of the liturgy. It holds together the unique work of each person of the Trinity with their togetherness in Love. Both the uniqueness and the belonging are different aspects of one Love. That symbolism helps people to affirm their own uniqueness whilst feeling that they belong to a wider community, reliving one of the struggles of being human.

Liturgy has an astringent quality: it provides a place that is trustworthy enough to take risks. The visions of God it mediates enhance both our uniqueness and our sense of belonging.

The notion of preventative care is seriously under-valued in our society. In institutions as disparate as the National Health Service and the Metropolitan Police, people prefer to react to 'disease' rather than take preventative action. The church's liturgy can be a powerful reminder that creating an environment of belonging is a fundamental task for a church concerned with the future health of humanity. Liturgy in numerous churches is almost the antithesis of such an environment. Conformity to the *status quo*, excluding the outsider, seems to be one of the clearest strategies in too many Christian congregations.

A third way in which liturgy functions as pastoral care is in creating an environment of *history and memory*. This is nowhere more vividly seen than in the Jewish liturgy of the Passover:

> Remembering with gratitude the redemption of our
>   fathers from Egypt,
> rejoicing in the fruits of our struggle for freedom,
> we look now with hope to the celebration of a future
>   redemption,
> the building of the City of Peace in which all men will
>   rejoice
> in the service of God, singing together a new song.[7]

All human groups need ways of dealing with the ambiguous depths of human life and particularly with their historic memories. Unlike the future, or even the present, the past is always given charged with its own ambiguous failures and successes. We need ways of dealing with that history which give us a sense of continuity and a personal identity. One of the toughest things about being human is our lack of choice about being born. Part of our inescapable heritage is our genetic patterning about which we had no choice. Mircea Eliade describes one of the functions of religion as the sober and serious coping with adaptation. Liturgy puts us in touch with the memory of who we are and our given-ness in order to adapt to the future given by Christ. It enables us to feel part of a history in which others have identified the same fundamental questions and discharged the same screams of terror against existence. Through it we also discover that today is not the end of the world.

Liturgy is an activity through which a community celebrates its values, passes on its norms and recreates a sense of its own identity through memory and forgiveness. Liturgy can be described, therefore, as an activity tied up with the complexities of human needs and motivations. Part of the ambiguity of all Christian experience is the attempt to hold human organisation and spiritual reality in a dynamic tension. Within that ambiguity, we are trying to make sense of our corporate memory. We are discovering our place and vocation within it so that we are free to create the future together with God. It is both the preservation and the expectation of hope.

That leads to a fourth way in which liturgy functions as care: it provides an environment for *telling the story*. Liturgy is a kind of passage from feeling to meaning. We all need to tell our own story in order to make sense of it, to make the links between past and present so that both may connect with the future. Our story is both unique and also the product of our common humanity. If it was only unique it would be unrecognisable, but because we are part of a common story we feel less alone. We belong to a community in which others have been sustained, restored and healed. We arrive from where we have been before. Anyone who has suffered bereavement, loss, failure, breakdown knows that it is vital to acknowledge the past story in order to embrace the future. In the sharing of our stories we hear the familiar echoes of failure and hope of unremarkable men and women. We discover that the tempest carries the seed of renewal.

But Christian liturgy also tells the story in a very particular way. It goes on retelling the story of Jesus because through that story we are to make sense of our own stories. If only we can connect his story and ours we shall begin to make sense. This is an important pastoral aspect of liturgy because in it we imitate the story of Jesus. This accounts to some extent for the careful precision that many demand of liturgical texts. It is a remembering and a re-doing of what Jesus did. The presence of Jesus is recreated through the liturgy.

Although there are many other factors in resistance to
liturgical change, which I will look at in the next chapter,
here at least is one. If this story of Jesus is a way of making
sense of our uniqueness and common stories, its represen-
tation in liturgy will be thought crucial for self-awareness.
Changing the way we tell it will sometimes be thought
controversial.

Carl Jung once wrote: 'The meeting of two personalities is
like the contact of two chemical substances: if there is any
reaction, both are transformed.'[8] I have never been happy
with the 'normal' definition of worship: i.e. giving worth or
respect to God. It has always seemed to me a too limited way
of describing what is essentially a dynamic process. I accept
that it is to God that ultimate worth is given, but I prefer the
definition of 'the mutual giving and receiving of worth'. That
as I understand it is what liturgy achieves at its best: it is
remarkably similar to what the quotation from Jung
describes. It is about transformation. On the one hand it
liberates me from my idols to attribute worth to the ultimately
personal, i.e. God. But I also discover that I am the recipient
of worth and value as I meet that God in worship. The case-
study with which we began focussed the central importance
of that. The idols of our society, like work, can strip people
of worth when they no longer have it. Old people feel worth-
less in a society which has lost any real sense of the value of
wisdom. That sense of worthlessness had been reinforced by
a distorted 'gospel' and in turn transformed by that elderly
group into 'bad news'. If liturgy, focussed on Jesus Christ, is
about the mutual giving and receiving of worth then it must
act directly as pastoral care because it confronts the basic
human need.
    There is a very powerful part of the Greek Orthodox liturgy
which illustrates this vividly. During the liturgy there is a
double movement of incense. First of all the saints who form
the iconostasis, i.e. the wall of icons, offer their adoration to
God through the offering of the incense. Then the thurifer
moves from the saints to the people and swings the incense
at them. This is followed by the people offering their adoration
to the saints by offering their adoration and love through the

incense. It is a marvellous image of the giving and receiving of worth.

The essence of pastoral care is the 'giving of unconditional positive regard to another' (Carl Rogers). The life experience of another person is worthy of loving attention, with all its contradictions. No matter how people regard themselves, they come to us as a gift. The typical activity of Jesus is the giving of worth to God and the receiving of worth from God. He is the focus and content of the liturgy. Liturgy is still more than that. It is a process through which each person is able to transcend their limited idols and give worth to the most High. We discover something given and we take hold of our own worth. Perhaps that is the only prerequisite for real worship: a willingness both to give and to receive worth because we have seen a flash of God. That flash of God is Jesus.

1. D. M. Thomas, *A White Hotel* (Penguin 1981), p. 218.
2. Christopher Bryant, *The Heart in Pilgrimage* (DLT 1980), p. 156.
3. W. A. Clebsch and R. C. Jaeckle, *Pastoral Care in Historical Perspective* (Harper, New York, 1967).
4. Don Browning, *The Moral Context of Pastoral Care* (Westminster Press 1976), pp. 108–9.
5. Dorothy Sayers, *The Just Vengeance* (Gollancz 1946), p. 24.
6. Douglas Davies, *The Broken Symbol* (British Association of Counselling, 1980).
7. *A Passover Haggadah* (Penguin 1978), p. 60.
8. Carl Jung, *Modern Man in Search of a Soul* (Routledge 1961), p. 57.

2

Walls of Resistance

Batter my heart, three person'd God; for you
As yet but knock, breathe, shine, and seek to mend;
That I may rise, and stand, o'erthrow me, and bend
Your force, to break, blow, burn and make me new.
(JOHN DONNE)

The following discussion was heard at a church council meeting:

VICAR: Well, now we come to the next item on the agenda, the sharing of the Peace at Holy Communion. Now as some of you are well aware this is a very common practice in very many churches today. I really feel that the time has come for us to begin here at St Peter's. I want to propose from the Chair that as from next month we begin the practice here.

(A long, uneasy silence followed.)

MR JONES: Well, vicar, as churchwarden I can safely say that the people won't wear it. You might – just might – get away with it at the 10 o'clock, but there's no way, no way at all, that those of us who come to the 8 are going to stand for it.

MRS ARBUTHNOT: Yes, I agree and I don't think we should have it at 10 o'clock either. We're there to give solemn worship to Almighty God not to shake each other by the hand. This trendy General Synod has got a lot to answer for.

MICHAEL JONES: Well, I was at the Methodist church with my fiancée a fortnight ago and everyone was cuddling each other. It was lovely . . . and there was a great sense of fellowship.

MRS POPE: Oh, I'd like a cuddle now and again (nervous laughter).

MR JONES: Oh yes! I remember when the vicar got us all to go to that 'charismatic' affair at the cathedral. It was like that then. One of the most dishonest events I've ever taken part in . . . there we were being asked to say 'Peace' when some of us were boiling inside.

MARJORIE GREEN: I had a funny feeling while that was going on. We were all supposed to be so friendly and warm to each other, but all I knew was that I hurt inside . . . don't know why, it was really peculiar. No, I don't want it started here. Not yet anyway.

PAUL EVERETT: But we're supposed to be a fellowship of the Holy Spirit. Surely that means reconciliation. Surely that is how it ought to be – sharing peace with each other.

MRS ARBUTHNOT: I agree but that's a spiritual thing . . . not a matter of . . . er . . . cuddling, as Mr Jones' young son put it. . . . Vicar there are many of us who will not have it. I'm sure people will start staying away and you know where that will put your diocesan quotas, don't you, vicar?

PAULINE SMITH: I go to church to be alone with God. I don't want lots of people invading my silence. It's the only time in the week I get away from the kids.

VICAR: Well, yes, er well, I think everybody has had a chance to express their views. I do think it would be so good for our fellowship together. Let's take a vote.

When the vote was taken, eleven voted against, six for the motion that the Peace should be shared. The motion was lost. The vicar moved immediately to the next item on the agenda.

Liturgy, which is the vehicle through which worship is expressed, needs to develop so that it can be true both to our intimations about God and our own changing self-understanding. Without growth, liturgy will quickly become archaic. It will fossilise into an old curiosity shop in which we have no further curiosity! But development and change, especially in liturgy, is almost bound to be met with resistance. Some of the characteristics of that resistance are already apparent in the discussion about the offering of the Peace: anger, hostility, disengagement, avoidance, denial, blocking, silence. They were all strategies being used by the group to resist a change that was clearly felt to be touching some powerful and difficult areas in their lives.

This is an area of liturgy in which insights derived from pastoral psychology may make an important contribution. There is a tendency within all the churches for people who resist change to be regarded as 'a pest' or as misguided, spiritually unsound, 'pig-headed' or just plain out of touch with contemporary realities. The controversy in the Anglican Church, involving a large number of public figures, about the 1662 Prayer Book has often been conducted at that kind of level. But here I would like to suggest an alternative approach to resistance. It may not finally resolve the problems but it might bring a different perspective to bear on them.

Within the allied disciplines of pastoral psychology, resistance is usually seen to be creative. It is not regarded as a bothersome hindrance or an insuperable obstacle to change. It is perceived as touching areas of human life which at the moment are felt to be either too 'hot' or too painful to handle. The presence of resistance can signify a creative area of reflection and action. Far from being 'a pest', it is likely to open up doors into new ways of seeing and being. It can be an exit to vision. If resistance is recognised as a gift to be treasured rather than an obstacle to change, it can begin to open up some areas of intimate relevance for the life of an individual or a group. If worship is in fact about opening up exits for vision, resistance may be one of its surest allies: 'To draw back before the object we are pursuing, only an indirect method is effective. We do nothing if we have not first drawn back. By pulling at the branch, we make all the grapes fall to the ground.' (Simone Weil)[1]

I want to take the arguments deployed by the protagonists in the above discussion as important clues to their difficulties about sharing the Peace. They represent insights about the motivations that bring people to worship as well as revealing matters of both importance and pain in their lives. We are asking a basic question that could be applied to any act of corporate worship: 'What's going on here?'

Let us begin with Pauline Smith's reaction about being 'alone with God'. The motivations that people bring to worship are very complex indeed. The problem with most of the books that have been written about worship is that they do not recognise that motives like 'getting away from the kids' are bound up with the longing to meet our 'Ground of Being and granite of it' (G. Manley Hopkins). But the complexity of the motivations deepens the human commitment and reinforces the resistance. But there is another important dimension to Pauline's resistance which we have already briefly touched on in chapter 1. She is saying something about the struggle for personal autonomy. Resistance is an important human strategy to establish our uniqueness. Pauline's protest about others invading her silence is an important statement about the need for aloneness. In psychotherapy the 'worker' needs to resist the 'assistant' (the therapist) in order to establish the boundaries of his or her life. All of us have blurred boundaries where we fail to distinguish between those things we want to take responsibility for and the voices within that are full of 'oughts' and 'shoulds' and 'be a good boy/girl'! Pauline was no doubt struggling with the boundaries of mother and child, wife and mother, lover and wife, mother and woman. The question is the first that God addressed to human beings: 'Where are you?

In trying to respond to that question, we battle to establish our own unique self against others and against God. The struggle for personal autonomy will always be like struggling with an angel (Genesis 32:22–32). For part of the dread of worship is that God will invade my territory and I will have no being left. When I was a university chaplain I found that part of my ministry was being a necessary adversary. Everyone needs to discover: 'I am, I see, and I feel that I am. And not only I am, but so I am, and so . . .'[2] There has to be a testing out against God as well as against other people to make that discovery. We need necessary adversaries. There are truths about ourselves that need protection from other people. If we believe that God desires our deepest good, then ultimately he will desire our uniqueness. It is a struggle for trust, and liturgy can provide a safe environment for that.

Pauline's withdrawal into silence with God is as much a marker of being a good mother as a search for wholeness, of which aloneness is a part. That is only one side of the Christian struggle, because we need to put our uniqueness at the service of others. But until we have discovered a sense of who we are, it is difficult to give to others without needing to possess them. Pauline's struggle to be a mother is just one indication of what was at stake in those few minutes in the church council. Henri Nouwen expresses this well:

> The mystery of love is that it protects and respects the aloneness of the other and creates the free space where he can convert his loneliness into a solitude that can be shared.
>
> In this solitude we can strengthen each other by mutual respect, by careful consideration of each other's individuality, by an obedient distance from each other's privacy and by a reverent understanding of the sacredness of the human heart.[3]

Mr Jones's comment about the 'charismatic' event indicates that worship can put us in touch with experiences which are potentially threatening whilst at the same time raising questions about truth and integrity. He is in one sense a gracious indication that the church is about its proper business. I say 'in one sense' because I do not want to underestimate that resistance which is the result of human sin; I will return to that later in the chapter. Meanwhile, there is a tendency in Christian churches to confuse the words 'conciliation' and 'reconciliation'. During the visit of the Pope to Britain in 1982, an ecumenical group suggested that celebrations of reconciliation should be held throughout the country. This was resisted by others in the ecumenical movement, including myself, on the grounds that such celebrations would have implied that the obstacles to unity had actually been removed. This was clearly not the current state of affairs in the relationships between the Roman Catholic and Protestant churches, and to have held celebrations suggesting that it was would have been a dishonest business.

A similar kind of instinct informs Mr Jones's comment, underlining an area of anxiety in many people's minds about the offering of the Peace. Whatever the objective theological reality, i.e. God has reconciled the world to himself, we frequently turn the promise of reconciliation into a lie. Issues of honesty and integrity are at stake, and we do no service to

anyone by pretending that they are not. Mr Jones felt a
gap between the internal and external worlds and knew that
something of great importance was at stake. He was in one
sense applying the acid test of apostolic faith. Did the quality
of life in the congregation actually reflect the objective fact of
faith, i.e. that we are reconciled to God and to each other in
Jesus? He felt that this was simply not the case. He was
fuming inside. He felt neither reconciled to himself nor to his
neighbour. This again raises an issue about preventative care.
If the quality of life in a congregation does not correlate to
some degree with statements of faith, that ambivalence needs
to be dealt with. There are occasions when men and women
will echo the prophet, Jeremiah:

> they dress my people's wound but skin-deep only,
>   with their saying, 'All is well.'
>   All well? Nothing is well![4]

It is interesting that the prophet actually relates the question
of integrity to healing and care. It corresponds to a conviction
among many lay people that claims for truth made in the
liturgy do not always correspond to facts.

Mr Jones' comment calls for some further examination of
the place of charismatic experience within liturgy. There is
little doubt that one of the major contributions of the charismatic movement to worship has been the opening up of liturgy
to the affective area of human personality. It has freed people
to express the joyful feelings of Pentecost. My difficulty with
charismatic worship is that it may have done that at the
expense of really confronting Golgotha. Although it enables
people to express good feelings, there is not a lot of evidence
in my experience of people being encouraged to face the
dark side. It may quite seriously arrest the journey towards
maturity, and I think there is now some evidence of that.
Since raising some critical questions about the Church of
England's evaluation of the charismatic movement in the
General Synod in 1981, I have received a number of letters
which have expressed something of the chaos and pain it
can bring to human lives. Charismatic liturgy, apart from
conventional appeals about sin and repentance, does not
always encourage that confrontation with the dark side which
enables people to integrate it. Like a lot of anaemic liturgy,

it may not always help people to engage in the cosmic battle between the opposites within themselves and within the world in order to make sense of them. Sometimes it does even deeper damage: in its more naive forms, it encourages the repression of that side of personality. I remember one student who became involved in the movement. Negative feelings had been repressed in his childhood: his involvement with the charismatic movement reinforced that. At the height of his involvement he stole £1,500 from the student union safe. In the end the dark side of his personality had to find expression somewhere.

But having said that, the charismatic movement could justly lay the charge that a great deal of conventional liturgy does not encourage the confrontation either. It would be quite right. For in a great deal of preaching and in many specially constructed acts of worship there is a split between the good and the dark aspects of personality. However, my particular struggle with the charismatic experience highlights a question about all liturgy. On the one hand I want to celebrate the liberating effect it has enabling people to express more of themselves in worship. But at the same time we need to question the suppression of dark feelings, for that not only arrests maturity in Christ but can contribute to serious break-down. It is an uneasy tension to live with and yet one which worship in many forms raises. There is no guarantee that worship will create the instant well-being of a person. It can lead to some deeply disturbing experiences.

Let us turn now to Marjorie Green and her conviction that 'all I knew was that I hurt inside'. There is a sense in which liturgy offers us a mirror image of ourselves, and our resist-ance can sometimes relate to that image. Mrs Pope's reaction parallels Marjorie Green's because both are hurting at some level, and so the Peace is seen as both potentially threatening and potentially liberating. It might be threatening because it is putting them in touch with feelings that they find difficult to deal with. It could be liberating because of the opportunity to do what they secretly wish to do, i.e. be cuddled. If liturgical innovation is resisted, it may offer some important clues to an individual's predicament. The Christian community is given an opportunity to reflect on the nature of resistance as a way into pastoral care. We shall look later in the chapter at strategies it might use to develop that.

Resistance can be a way of avoiding both God, who might be able to heal, and myself, who would prefer not to take responsibility for my hurt self. The Peace can confront us with the poverty of not having fulfilling relationships in the rest of our lives. It has a way of exposing a broken marriage, the breakdown of relationships between parents and children, loneliness and lack of human comfort, a sense of being unfulfilled in a career or job or sexual frustration. There may be many other areas, sometimes unconscious, which the offering of the Peace exposes. It can strip us temporarily of our masks, exposing our vulnerability or sense of worthlessness or just the wilderness inside, which we do not understand. It has a way of discerning the spirits. If the psyche draws on our collective history for its strength, there is an important sense in which it will also carry echoes of both the comedy and tragedy of that history. The declaration of the Peace will confront those bits of collective suffering that have found a lodging place in us. We may, therefore, be highly resistant to the exposure of both the breadth and depth of that pain: 'and all the past, inaccessibly calling' (Terence Tiller).

I turn finally to Mrs Arbuthnot, who expresses resistance in the classic form. As we have observed the behaviour of some of the other participants in our case study, it has become clear that liturgy is one way of dealing with some of the ambiguous depths of our relationships, human and divine. Resistance can be a way of avoiding getting too close to either human or divine reality. It brings us close to a classic understanding of how worship functions as an essential element in human life.

Liturgy expresses to some degree both the conflicts and hopes of humanity. It puts people in touch with those forces that they feel are potentially destructive as well as their springs of hope. But it also stops people going mad. The depths of life can be experienced as both creation and destruction. Liturgy provides a structure in which people are helped to deal with those ambiguous realities. In our recent collective history, the example of Nazi Germany demonstrates what happens when one set of symbols goes dead. Other archetypes can hold sway plunging a whole nation into its demonic

depths. Individuals and groups need ways of dealing with the
depths of life without them becoming destructive. They also
need a safe framework within which to encounter what Mrs
Arbuthnot calls 'Almighty God': the Almighty can be experienced as deeply threatening as well. Many priests, as
representatives of God, know the very powerful pulls of people
wanting to be close and yet keeping their distance because
holiness is felt to be untouchable and, therefore, threatening.

This process can, of course, be highly ambiguous. People
can use worship as a means of living in a maternal cocoon.
It is quite possible to regard the church's worship as existing
for nostalgic trips back to childhood or opportunities to play
Father's 100 Best Tunes! Dependent faith is as much an
enemy of true faith as more familiar heresies:

> The Christian life is a continual process of leaving the
> Church as an institution ... as that which does our
> thinking, praying and even loving for us – yes, the Church
> as Mother. But the Christian way is also a continued redis-
> covering of the Church as a community in which it is
> possible for persons to be freed and healed ... it is easy to
> forget that, when my friend touches me, there is the Church
> in action.   (A. Jones)[5]

Our resistance can touch the ambiguous desire both to be in
touch with the depths of God and to protect ourselves from
that. Most people who worship have an intuition that God's
love can be a disconcerting, if not profoundly disturbing,
experience. Liturgy can protect us against that disconcerting
encounter. At the same time it can offer the means to make
sense of our intuitions of love.

The fastidiousness that some people bring to liturgy, as
well as the kind of resistance that Mrs Arbuthnot shows, is
an attempt to deal with that level of ambiguous feeling. Even
her threat of people withdrawing is a pastorally perceptive
comment, for people do withdraw into themselves, away from
others, when they are in contact with threatening experiences.
If the Peace opens up the way to our being touched not just
by another person but by God's love, which both purges and
heals, then we may well want to do everything in our power
to avoid such a disturbing encounter.

It would, nevertheless, be an illusion to argue that all

resistance is pastorally valuable, because that would be based on a distorted view of human nature. Few of us will not have met areas in ourselves, let alone in others, which are extraordinarily resistant to change and development. Despite our complex activities to change individuals and situations, resistance can remain as impervious as ever. The resistance to new ways of seeing reality is rooted in some of the darker realms of our unconscious life: what is required is a more truthful perception of the human condition. We are up against hard realities which are part of our common human predicament. They are indicators of the need for the mercy of God which puts all our projects, even liturgy, into their true perspective:

> The myriad resistances large and small that challenge, undermine, and frustrate our ministries at every turn are therefore expressions of the central human dilemma which ministry is all about and are not mere impediments on the way to something else.   (R. Hunter)[6]

All these responses are then part of what it means to encounter the living God in worship. Because they illustrate dilemmas about being human, I have tried to make the case that resistance is a pastoral opportunity for a community's growth in self-knowledge and mutual understanding. We need to look now at some of the alternative strategies that a Christian community might use in dealing with such resistance. How could the Christian community facilitate a real meeting with resistance that would promote growth? I am suggesting that this is the responsibility of the Christian community, because it seems to me that one further point of resistance in the church council discussion was the feeling that this was an attempt at clerical domination rather than an opportunity to regard liturgy as 'the work of the People of God'. The responsibility for promoting real health in liturgy must be a collective one. Priests and ministers do not own worship, even though they may act some of the time as though they do. If a priest feels that the only thing that he was ordained to do is to celebrate the Christian Eucharist he can, in fact, never forget that he does that on behalf of others. Authorised minis-

tries are a reminder to the people of God of their vocation in
ministry and mission.

Because of the tendency of many clergy to believe that the
ordering of liturgy is their sole responsibility, it is not impossible to envisage a situation where an 'appropriate' strategy
might have been to ignore the church council and simply to
initiate change on the basis of clerical authority alone. Such
a manoeuvre is not unthinkable in either the Roman Catholic
or Anglican churches. I hope that the diagnosis of this chapter
will have persuaded some that such a strategy would not only
be liturgically ineffective but also pastorally damaging. At the
very least it would be a missed pastoral opportunity.

A second, and more sophisticated, version of that strategy
would be for the minister to change the form of the liturgy.
The Peace, for example, might be introduced in a very
restrained form like the president of the Eucharist sharing it
with the deacon or chief server. An extended form of that is
a formal exchange at the Peace by 'designated' ministers
down the central aisle of the church; a kind of offering by
remote control! The risk is that a priest becomes a tinkerer
with liturgy. If the priest abdicates his central role for that
of managing things better he or she becomes part of the
problem. We have acknowledged that innovation in worship
can be a vital source of renewal and growth but 'fiddling
about' with the liturgy can be a way of evading reality. Priests
may have to face serious questions about their own delusions
of power if they believe that they can manage change through
liturgical innovation against the *mysterium tremendum* of human
personality.

A third strategy, based again on traditional patterns of
power, would be to mount a catechetical programme to help
people understand the correct theology, traditions and meanings within worship. There is, however, little evidence that
traditional patterns of education based on the notion of a
package deal in which knowledge is transmitted from one
party to another actually changes human behaviour. It is also
clear that what we are dealing with are not 'rational'
responses amenable to Western educational systems. Even if
the behaviour of resistance at first seems meaningless judged
by the usual educational criteria, all behaviour has meaning
if we test it against the criteria of analytical psychology. It

not only has meaning but the facts are ultimately friendly. It would seem, therefore, that a didactic or catechetical approach to resistance does not really face the basic problem.

A fourth strategy might have a number of elements in it, based primarily on the conviction that resistance is best dealt with by being brought into focus. The Christian community is about preparing the ground for disclosure moments. The attention of that community needs to be captured so that people recognise that they are dealing with a problem that is neither insurmountable nor unable to be discussed. Part of the difficulty with the church council's debate was that there was no real discussion. Everyone's opinion was heard but there was no meeting between the people expressing the opinions. It is the result of one of the major products of Protestantism, 'the inner-directed character'[7] (see also chapter 1). The resistance was ignored or despaired about. Certainly attacking it head on, which would have been another all too familiar strategy, would only have reinforced the resistance.

One way in which real dialogue can begin is for the priest or minister to express some of the reasons why he or she might resist change and innovation. Expressing his or her own inner conflict may help others to identify some of the same areas of darkness within themselves. 'Yes, I find myself in your words . . .' This approach presupposes that something is being touched upon which affects our corporate humanity and it can become an opportunity to help a congregation to look at resistance in order to work through it.

Another version of that is to 'act out' some of the resistance. One of the ways in which we resist facing God, others and ourselves is to turn up late. I can think of one church in a multi-racial area where the Eucharist is scheduled for 10.00 a.m. The vicar never turns up before 10.15 and the service rarely starts before 10.35! They say, 'We keep West Indian time here.' But there seems to be an inescapable resistance. It may be about different races finding it painful to meet each other or about a cultural conditioning which has led to believing in a God of terror. One way of dealing with this situation is for everyone to begin turning up late including the vicar (which in this case was no problem!) and then for someone to raise the question, 'I wonder why it is that we never begin worshipping God on time?' An acted parable often has greater power than any words.

A third way would be to take a genuinely educational approach. Opportunities could be created to work through the real problems of resistance through the use of case studies and role-plays, or by discussion of actual pastoral situations. The discussion would have to be pursued in an environment of genuine openness with no hidden agenda, e.g. to get this congregation to accept the Peace. The case-study with which this chapter began would make a useful starter for discussion. The educational aim must be to draw out of the people present their own difficulties about liturgical innovation in worship. This will happen only if people know from the beginning that there will be an honest acceptance of their difficulties and a warm recognition of why 'I hurt inside'. This kind of educational activity needs to be based on tough encouragement and the community's pastoral intuitions. Education is about reflecting on experience in a way that leads to new and creative actions. That is remarkably different from what passes in numerous parishes and churches for adult education. In the end the truth of Christianity is an event which goes on happening in the heart of human life. It is about a new revelation that leads to a place that none of us have been to before.

The vision of God can be a deeply disturbing experience: it can face us with choices about our ultimate loyalty and our deepest dread. The vision of God, who reconciles all things and all people into a new kind of co-inherence, challenges our comfortable hopelessness, in which we rest content with a stereotype of ourselves. It is no wonder that we resist such a vision. But knowing the truth about ourselves and facing its implications may ultimately free us. In the short term we resist because it can cause what feels like infinite pain. But if our diagnosis is correct, that resistance is in fact the passage from feeling to meaning. Worship puts us in touch with threatening and liberating truths. Resistance to them is almost invariably a moment of pastoral opportunity and potential growth. They are occasions for Christians to minister to each other so that reconciliation might be not only declared fact but also assured hope. They are times when we wait expectantly for the coming of God in the centre of our pains. Many experiences of unfulfilment may remind us of God's absence but the paradox is that he knows the walls with which we protect ourselves. By waiting for his word of reconciliation we can slowly break through each other's illusory walls. In the end the word of reconciliation lifts us up beyond the boundaries of our existence to the One whose anarchic mercy restores our valued integrity to us. We offer that to one another in the Peace.

1. Simone Weil, *Gravity and Grace* (Routledge 1952), p. 106.
2. From *The Cloud of Unknowing*.
3. Henri Nouwen, *Reaching Out* (Fount 1980), p. 44.
4. Jeremiah, 6:14 (NEB)
5. Alan Jones, *Journey into Christ* (SPCK 1977), p. 110
6. Rodney Hunter, 'Ministry or Magic?', *Princeton Seminary Bulletin* (New Series 1977), vol. 1, pp. 61–7.
7. See D. W. Smythe 'Some Observations on Communication Theory' in *Sociology of Mass Communications* (ed. D. McQuail, Penguin Books 1972), p. 27.

3

The Altar of the World

The Body of Christ becomes for you an altar. It is more holy than the altar of stone on which you celebrate the holy sacrifice. You are able to contemplate this altar everywhere, in the street and in the open squares. (ST JOHN CHRYSOSTOM)

The Christian Eucharist is an open invitation to the world of the imagination. Few Christians today would deny that the Eucharist is their central drama. In it we explore both the destruction that is unleashed when our false illusions are exposed, and the wonder of rediscovering the truth of who we are. Pastoral care can offer us skills to explore those depths and heights of human experience. One of those skills is the 'fantasy journey'. By taking an imaginary journey through the world of the Eucharist we may discover great clues as to who we are. There is no way that you can get such a journey right or wrong. It is unique. But fifteen years of pastoral counselling has taught me that my unique journey has many collective aspects. I am going, therefore, to risk sharing this journey in the hope that my vulnerability will help others to explore the profundity of the Eucharist.

I was in a typical London street. It was lined with London plane trees, their branches winter-bare. Most of the houses had suffered from the ravages of time. A bitter wind blew a front page of the *Daily Mirror* against my legs. The headline simply said: 'No Exit'. I heard someone running behind me. A small, mongoloid girl caught up with me and grabbed my hand. We walked on. We saw a man walking towards us. His hair was unkempt but silver grey. He wore what looked like

an academic gown but one sleeve was torn in shreds. Behind
him jogged a young man in a bright red track suit. A black
woman crossed the road towards us. She was crying tears of
blood.

We met near a door in the wall. It was a round arch
engraved with geometric patterns. I pushed the door. It
creaked open. I went in. The others followed. The door led
into a small room. The walls were grey. In one corner a man
sat with his back towards us. He was wearing a grey uniform.
In front of him was a small machine. It was covered with
flashing lights. On the table beside him was a large black box
marked 'the ultimate zone'. His finger was on a button. It
said 'Nuclear first strike'. He swung round towards us. He
was faceless. I let go of the little girl's hand and fled towards
a hole in the wall.

It led into a dimly lit passage. I ran down in. It was wet
and cold and the further I went the steeper it became. It was
dark and I tripped over what looked like a heap of rags. I
crawled towards it. A hand stretched out. It was black. I saw
her face. It was covered with dried blood. A voice echoed
down the corridor: 'Brixton . . . remember Soweto, remember
the whip in your hand on the slave gallery . . .' I was almost
numb with the cold but I rushed on. The corridor became
more and more serpentine. I found myself in a large cave
with a great pool of water. I stared into it. The water was
hideously clear and black serpents swam in it. Floating in the
same water were bodies of babies. I heard weeping. A
Japanese man sat chained in a corner. He was covered with
terrible burns. He said: 'You gave me everything except
tomorrow.' I looked into the water again. As if in a mirror a
hideous snake stared back at me.

I entered the water. Inside were some steps. I walked down
until the waters covered me. The darkness was total. I was
out of my depth. I looked again. Out of the darkness two
forms appeared. They wore militia-style grey uniforms and
had guns at their belts. They guarded another staircase. I
approached. They tried to stop me. They, too, were faceless
and they had no words. I said to them: 'This is the way.' I
began to climb the steps.

On my way up I heard a child reading. He had a large
book in his hands, bound with leather and ribbed with filigree

brass. I heard him whisper: 'This is the word of the Lord.' Then out of the book he took a towel and beckoned me towards him. He began to dry me. I realised for the first time that I was naked. Then he offered me the towel to cover my nakedness.

I climbed on up the spiral staircase. There was a large stone shelf and beside it another door. On the shelf was a Pieta carved out of the stone of the wall. The figures were only half formed. They struggled to be free of the stone. I discerned the form of a woman. As I looked great drops of blood fell from her eyes. I stared at the door. On it were carved the words: A place to stand. I pushed it and went in.

In the middle of the room a huge globe stood on a wooden table. I stood and began to move it gently with my hands. As it revolved large cracks began to appear in it. Out of the cracks flowed streams of blood. I continued to hold it in my hands. I peered into the cracks. In one I saw a great ecclesiastical assembly with many arms raised. I heard a voice: 'The motion to covenant in unity is lost.' The raised arms looked momentarily like clenched fists. In another crack I saw a queue of people dressed in night clothes, their hands held out for their night-time drug. I looked into another – a tiny baby lay in an incubator its limbs twisted and disfigured; a father stood close by staring into space. In another I saw a young woman lurching towards a man, a carving knife gripped in her hand. In another a frail man lay in bed, his hand clasping his heart. But as I peered I saw a glow of golden light in the heart of the globe. Slowly it filled the whole globe from inside and the cracks began to close. I held the globe in my hands and stood very still. Then I looked down at the floor.

It was circular and made of mosaic. In the middle, underneath the table, was an inner circle. As I looked down the wooden crosspiece at the base of the table filled the inner circle. The circular mosaic was divided into seven sections. I walked round it. In the first section a young black man stared through prison bars. But as his hands gripped the bars in hopeful defiance, they began to crack. In the second a woman was removing a black hood and running towards a man who was tearing off a high clerical collar. Both had blood on their hands. They were in a Belfast street. In the next one a woman and a man stood shoulder to shoulder: one held up a silver cup; the other a broken loaf of bread. In the fourth a circle of children danced round another globe. They trampled on a pile of missiles. In the fifth segment a pair of wounded hands were cupped and stretched out. In the cupped hands was a large pearl. I walked round to the sixth. In it was a tree. It grew inside a pointed arch but its branches broke through the arch and stretched upwards and outwards. At the foot of the tree sat a man embracing another man. I reached the seventh. The body of a bishop lay slumped across an altar, blood pouring from a gun wound. The blood streamed over the altar, down the aisle and out through a door. Through the door a man in a militia uniform was clubbing a young woman with a large stave. The sub-tropical sun beat down. I glanced up at the ceiling and read the words, 'Seventy times seven'.

I turned, went back to the staircase and climbed again. It opened out into a huge city square surrounded by high buildings covered with inscriptions. I was drawn towards a corner of the square, where I recognised the man in the academic gown, the woman with tears of blood, the young man behind the prison bars, the Japanese man without his chains, the man with the red track suit, and many others. They stood around an altar of stone. On it lay the mongoloid girl. As I looked she stood up and stepped down. She was a young woman with no trace of mongoloid features. She took a piece of bread and broke it and offered it to everyone present. Then she lifted a cup and handed it round. As her hands offered it to me I saw in each of them a healed wound.

I turned and saw the arched door through which I had come. I walked out through it. The London plane trees were full of fresh green buds. Through a window of one of the houses, a man smiled. I realised it was me.

Before reading on, it might be helpful to pause and reflect on what you have experienced as you shared that journey with me. Some parts of it may have been disturbing or distressing: others parts may be enigmatic and puzzling.

With the help of that imaginary journey I want now to reflect on our corporate human experience as we share in this great drama of Love, through which we believe all creation and all humanity is restored to its true destiny in God. As I reflect on it I want also to draw out some practical consequences for the celebration of the Eucharist.

Liturgy makes it possible for each person to appropriate that truth about themselves in their own way. We carry to the liturgy not only the sights and sounds and reflections of everyday things. We carry also the prayers of others. But there is another sense in which we appropriate this truth. In the liturgy everyone is able to make a response. The mongoloid girl and the academic who came face to face at the door would both be able to respond to God in their own way with the signs and symbols, the colours and the music of the liturgy. The liturgy is like this because it has that universality which proclaims that we are not alone. It is both universal and holistic in its approach to truth. One of the most exhausting fantasies of being Christian is that 'we are here to be good'. The preservation of that fantasy is a draining business, and many Christian congregations are trapped in a conspiracy to preserve it. But the liturgy rightly appropriated is about nothing of the kind. We can risk being unique, tearing down the walls that are the symbols of our self-protection. Why is the liturgy like this? Partly because it has the inherent power to draw women, children and men – irrespective of intellect, emotional security, education, class, sexual orientation – into a new way of being. It does not matter where we come from. At some level of being, we are able to understand what is going on. We should come to know ourselves more profoundly. It may also deepen our recognition of pain and hope.

That understanding is an important form of care. In a society which functions around the differences between people, the liturgy becomes a symbol of a world based on radically different expectations:

> In word and act, Jesus rejects the world's rejections, and causes the rejected to be accepted. In his sharing of food with the tax-collectors and sinners, he creates for them a new relation with each other and with God by bringing them into relationship with himself. (R. Williams)[1]

There are immediate practical implications. The first is obvious. The Christian community can never be uniform in its social make-up. One of the joys of inner-city life is to experience the power of liturgy in this way. The second is this. Many people will need support in preparing for the Eucharist, a time of recollection in which to in-gather and focus the whole of their life into this act of communion. It focusses the essence of Christian spirituality, the development of our whole life in a God-ward direction, and becomes, therefore, an acid test of the spiritual life of the whole congregation.

But there are some even more down-to-earth implications. If people are to appropriate worship in their way they can be helped by that desire to worship being unhindered. Elderly people whose eyesight is failing would be greatly helped by having large-print texts. People will also be helped if they have clear, straightforward texts to follow. It does not help to receive two hymnbooks, a hymn sheet, a news-sheet, a liturgical text and this congregation's variations on it when arriving in church. I think we underestimate how we intimidate people who are trying to find their way back into God. It may be difficult for handicapped people to worship simply because they can't get in to where its happening. Ramps, large-type texts and simple liturgical forms are some symbols of how serious we are about worship being for everyone. In Jesus' day, the handicapped were banned from the Temple: the ban seems to have been lifted in theory rather than in reality.

The Church has domesticated sin. In the early part of my imaginary journey I had to face some of my own dark depths. Those depths were inhabited by a faceless man with his finger on the switch of nuclear catastrophe, the broken body of a black woman and a Japanese man without a tomorrow. It was an intimation that I acquiesce in destructive evil and also inherit the consequences of an evil past. The depths of my collective guilt are beyond me. It is no response to that guilt simply to invite confession and penitence in personal and individualistic terms. We need to take responsibility for our own self-illusions and to find release from them. But we do not live in a moral vacuum, impervious to the consequences of the past or the corporate illusions of the present. We are diminished by our collusion with the powers of darkness:

> By discovering my past of oppression, I can discover my own self-diminution in the process; and in pressing back to the source of this vicious spiral, I discover the primary lack of wholeness, the primary deprivation, which is part of belonging to the single human story.   (R. Williams)[2]

If there is an element of mutual deprivation and violence, which the notion of individual responsibility cannot adequately deal with, that needs to be taken account of in the liturgy. The phenomenon of corporate complicity in mutual violence needs a corporate response.

I am not convinced that contemporary rites of confession and absolution do sufficient justice to our corporate complicity. The older rites were almost obsessional in their preoccupation with human sin and worthlessness. The Reformation rites took it a stage further by harnessing that to an individualistic view of salvation. But both had a more honest perspective on our mutual displacement through violence and illusion than the apologetic new rites. That shift seems to mirror a fundamental shift in the whole of Western society. It is the shift from a corporate to a private way of living.

But that need not intimidate us. The practice of corporate confession and absolution can be set in a context in which our corporate collusion with the forces of oppression and annihilation is openly acknowledged. One way of achieving that is to develop periods of silence in the eucharistic liturgy, for all worship is a waiting upon God for moments of disclosure. The use of silence prior to an act of confession can help individuals not only to focus their own loss of freedom and responsibility but also their conspiracy with 'things ill done and done to others' harm' (T. S. Eliot). That waiting needs to call up the power of memory about our responsibilities in a world where many are dying of starvation. Tissa Balasuriya says of this: 'The Eucharist is in captivity. It is dominated by persons who do not experience oppression in their own selves.'[3]

The oppressor always runs two risks. The first is that of making the victim guiltless. The second is to internalise the oppression until it numbs all sense of corporate responsibility.

Both are illusions perpetuated by a Western Church which all too often lines up with the oppressor. Worship cares for us when it releases those of us who live under the illusion of dominance from its insidious power. We are cared for when we are confronted with a proper sense of our own limitations.

In one single action of confession and absolution our anxiety about being separate is heightened and the security of being part of one humanity is strengthened. We bring the guilt about who we are, the fractured relationships that words would not heal, our share in the corporate darkness of injustice and evil, our recognition that healing is the vocation of a lifetime. We know that here at least God's reconciling and healing love can be made real. In this great prelude of restoration, we recognise our mutual collusion in darkness and deceit. Pastoral care is always about our illusions being stripped away so that we can take a fuller responsibility for our lives. The ministry of absolution mediates that depth of care. We are invited to turn round and face the future so that we can begin shaping that future according to Christ's gift of new humanity. Christ always comes to a waiting people from his new future.

That highlights another practical concern. We have lost the art of catechesis in the contemporary Church. I do not wish the old catechism to be revived, but I do want to belong to a learning and growing community in which we rediscover the meaning of baptism, and therefore of confession and absolution. We need to become a catechetical Church in which more time and resources are given to education and discovery. We need to enlarge this radical meeting of human experience and Christian orthodoxy; a practising of getting out of depth in the depths of the world's darkness, knowing that a word of absolution always lies beyond. It is no coincidence that in my imaginary journey I found myself completely out of my depth at the bottom of the pool of water. Lay Christians need infinitely more encouragement in making connections between penitence and absolution in the Monday-to-Saturday world. It is that broken world that is offered to God for restoration and right relationships in the Eucharist.

I would now like to link the question of catechesis to the

ministering of the word of God. In the first chapter I spoke of
worship creating an environment of meaning. In my journey a
small child opened a book and read. He also drew a towel
from it. I remember a day when the phone rang at a particularly inconvenient time. 'What do you think about abortion?'
'Er, well, I haven't given it much thought recently . . .'
'Listen, you're a priest and I'm talking about me.' The friend
went on to explain that she had had superb counselling about
her problem but there had been questions that the counselling
service had found unanswerable. At that moment she needed
help in setting the decision, which she still had to take and
which could never be 'right', in a much larger frame of reference. She talked of murder and blood sacrifice, of crucifixion
and what could be called 'the Sabbath of creation' (Saunders
Lewis). I saw her on several occasions and we talked about
how her decision might look from God's point of view.
Pastoral care and counselling can take you so far but sometimes that needs to be set within a wider context. I am
suggesting that the ministry of the Word begins to provide
such a structure, but numerous Christians will need further
help with 'two-legged walking', walking on the Word and the
world.

That highlights the responsibility of those who minister
that Word. I shall devote a whole chapter later to preaching
and teaching (see chapter 8); at this point I shall deal with
the reading of Scripture. Those people who read the Scriptures have a responsibility to mediate a word of hope. Where
care is taken about how the Scriptures are read there tends
to be an over-emphasis on voice production and pronunci-
ation. All that is necessary, but equal attention does not seem
to be given to understanding the texts being read. One of the
secrets of pastoral care is the quiet preparation of listening
and attentiveness that goes on before and after any pastoral
encounter. We listen for the words John or Mary didn't say.
A similar discipline needs to be developed with the ministry
of the Word. Numerous groups gather for Bible study but
very few groups exist for those who minister the word of God.
It would be a helpful discipline in many congregations for
those who have the responsiblity of reading the Scriptures to
meet once a month to reflect on what they will read. That
could be shared imaginatively with those who exercise the

priestly ministry of intercession. The context of such a ministry is 'deep calling to deep', even to the depths of my friend's blood-sacrifice. *The word of God is a towel of service.*

Let us look at the globe that cracked open. Intercession is about standing in the presence of God believing that all behaviour has meaning. Psychological insights are vital to our corporate praying. They offer us a vision of that inner struggle towards maturity which is part of paying loving attention to God. In intercession we are affirming that this particular litany of the human journey has ultimate meaning. We are caring for others in a number of ways. We are recognising that human autonomy is not the measure of all care. Intercession is an activity of judgement because it calls the bluff on my subtle desires to be omnicompetent. It is also an activity of hope because it opens up the possibility of another person being completed beyond themselves. We do not worship a limp and idealised picture of ourselves. We need this mysterious and prophetically pastoral focus to our worship as a reminder that we are co-creators with God. Intercession is the work of co-creation: 'Through the Eucharist we are extensions of Christ's vulnerability, sustained by the food of his victory: we are not guards placed at the door of his anteroom to protect him from profanation or contact with the world' (A. Vagel).[4]

Intercession raises issues about the ultimate meaning of all our behaviour. In it our understanding of divine providence and its relationship to human pain and opportunity is put to its surest test. Intercession is the focus around which we rebuild our defences against doubt or we stand in the presence of God trusting his good purposes. The lectures to God that we hear so often at this stage of the Eucharist are little more than a sign of deep mistrust. I shall never forget the three-minute obituary notice that God heard on the Sunday after Joyce Grenfell's death – God does not need to be told all the facts! Intercession can be a means of enlarging the fantasy that we can control God. When it becomes that, it is heresy. Intercession at its best is our affirming the good purposes of God in the whole universe, even if they cannot be fathomed.

But tested against pastoral criteria that may raise some very difficult issues about public prayer.

We could spend a few moments reflecting on how we would pray in these pastoral contexts:

(a) A gynaecological ward in a general hospital where a ward service happens every other week. Some of the patients have had abortions, others hysterectomies. Other patients will probably be unable to have children.

(b) The woman minister has confided in you that she is gay. The church committee has recently discussed a report on 'Homosexual Relations' and has issued a statement to the congregation condemning all gay relationships.

(c) The vicar's wife has had her first child and you know it is a spina-bifida birth.

(d) The local authority is proposing to build a hostel for ex-prisoners on the site opposite the church. They bought the land from the church under a compulsory purchase order.

(e) Peter, a single man recently discharged from psychiatric care, is being kept alive on a life-support machine after being injured in a road accident.

Our pastoral care raises ethical and moral perspectives which need testing against an objective historical and theological frame of reference. (I have already discussed this in chapter 1 with reference to the different human models which influence pastoral care.) Intercession encourages both the expression and the containment of powerful feelings related to pastoral events. But that participation means that those who lead intercession may need to work hard at the criteria of what is offered in public prayer.

Intercession underlines, too, the continuity between care and prayer, and time needs to be given to its preparation. Intercession is understood in the New Testament as a priestly ministry. It has a double movement. It is about entering the depths of the human predicament, and it is also about standing before God holding those predicaments in stillness. As Alan Eccelestone expresses this: 'Because creation

proceeded afresh every day prayer must be a new scanning
of the scene with a readiness to discern what God was about.'5

But the mosaic of liberation and restoration also underlines
the social significance of making Eucharist together. The
Eucharist is concerned with the transformation of material
structures, and there is a proper continuity between the world
as it is and the city of God. The Peace sets our personal pain
within a social context of reconciliation: the reconciliation of
the whole created order and the whole of humanity to God.
It offers release from the oppressions that damage us as people
and challenges the contemporary political heresies that
human beings are only to be valued for what they own and
possess. The myths that lie at the heart of many contemporary
economic-political theories in Britain are challenged by the
Christian Eucharist. The Peace declares that human beings
are not means to an end. When human beings worship, their
true self is restored to them individually and socially. Worship
is, therefore, an end in itself and by its very nature the most
radical critique of every political ideology.

The Peace mediates care in another important way. As it
holds out a vision of human liberation, it nurtures a
compassion for all human beings. Without that love, the
search for social justice can become another form of
oppression because our motives are not purified. Forgiveness
is about the liberation of both the oppressed and the oppressor
in and through loving reconciliation. Mercy in worship and
in pastoral care knows no frontiers.

Worship is about the desire to be whole. Carl Jung describes
the great eucharist prayer as 'the rite of the individuation
process'.6 It is a well observed psychological process in many
cultures that self-knowledge comes mainly through suffering.
The eucharistic offering is about that transformation taking
place. It is an environment in which we participate in the
suffering and resurrection of Christ. We are placed on the
altar and claim our darkness and our light as part of God's
ordering of the universe. Our complex psychological forces
begin to find a focus in the symbols of bread and wine. Those
symbols signify both the suffering of God and his dominion
over the universe. Through sharing in them we are recog-

nising both our fractured self, the dark side of ourselves, and our desire to be whole. The transformation of the mongoloid girl into the woman priest in the imaginary journey is one way of trying to speak of this Easter reality.

Jung was perplexed about the extent to which the Christian Christ could adequately be the symbol of the self because of the ways in which Christian orthodoxy had insisted that Christ was all light. He seemed to Jung to represent the repression of the dark side of human nature. It made the approximation of our actual experience to Christ that much more difficult. I think that Jung may have underestimated two significant features of what he called our 'participation mystique' in the symbolism of the Mass. First of all Christ can only be for us by first being against us. That seems to be a basic principle of both worship and pastoral care. It may seem like a strange reversal to much conventional pastoral wisdom but I believe it squares with experience. When I share my pain with another, they represent to me the possibility of another way. It is the possibility of being healed by entering more deeply into the pain. There are times when to encounter the living Christ is to feel perplexed, hateful, fearful, violent or destructive. Christ exposes the dark side of ourselves. Communion or *participation mystique* with him can only be real if we can share that darkness so that it can be accommodated through healing. It is part of the genius of the Christian gospel that we stay with pain, however profoundly it hurts, even into the depths of 'the grave of the trembling universe' (Saunders Lewis). Too much that is claimed in the name of Christian healing is an evasion of that pain. The healing focussed at the centre of the Eucharist is one of confrontation with our darkness so that we can find release even if it leads to vulnerability.

The second significant feature that Jung underestimates is the fact that the Host is fractured. He recognises it but does not appear to work out its full implication: 'The connection between this and the sacrificial death of Christ lies in the descent into hell and the breaking of the infernal power. The breaking of the bread that now follows is symbolic of Christ's death.'[7]

The self is focussed not only in the whole Host but in the fractured Host. On the cross Christ is the person that I dare not be. He represents, therefore, to me that shadow side of myself. But on the cross, he represents more than that. The fracturing is the taking upon himself the burden of human darkness which has accumulated in the abyss of many centuries. There is an identification of the One at the centre fractured and broken by my darkness and my consciousness of that darkness:

> What we are refusing is not, directly at least, 'obedience to God' but some fulness of life to which God is impelling us and which our whole being dreads. Some unbearable personhood, identity, freedom, whose demands beat on our comfortable anonymity and choice of death. Further, something that at root we are, a self that is ours yet persistently ignored in favour of the readily satisfiable needs of the ego. (S. Moore)[8]

In the eucharistic centre I am able to be my unique self.

I want to relate this to a further aspect of Jung's thought. He focusses the sacrificial aspect of the great eucharistic prayer in the notion of gathering together the scattered parts of ourselves. The process of becoming human is represented by the putting together of all those fragmented elements that have stopped us from being human. We become ourselves by taking possession of all that we are, for it is only the person who is in possession of him/herself who can give themselves away. I recollect reflecting on this process at the time of the breakdown of my marriage. My spiritual director had told me to stay in the marriage as a sacrifice. My response was that I might have the right to sacrifice myself but I did not have the right to sacrifice either my children or my wife. But I was not even in posession of all the fractured parts of my self. I was not free to make my sacrifice. I dreaded becoming more conscious of myself but my self drove me towards even deeper suffering. Only God, it seemed, could be both the sacrificer and the sacrificed gift.

We are caught up into a movement through which we catch a glimpse of our wounded self being restored by that sacrificial gift. There is in this eucharistic prayer a structure, sometimes constricting, sometimes liberating, but always holding the possibility of continuing community. I can acknowledge in and through it some of my deepest darkness and inarticulate dread. The circle of our consciousness is widened and the threatening dread of remaining alone is abolished for ever. But there is another important sense today in which we need to be kept in touch with the lust for blood and destruction which we vented on Jesus.

The passionate and irrational god of violence and frenzy is able to take possession of human hearts and drive them into the fantasy of universal destruction. Christianity has too often sterilised that aspect, preferring its domesticated panaceas to a frank confrontation with the god of war who can violently possess the unconscious life of whole nations. Part of what I call the astringent nature of liturgy may be the honest containment of those terrifying demands. It can offer an objective frame of reference which permits us to plumb those depths but with hope. Christianity can collude with repressing the archetypal forces or it can encourage their actualisation. It has a grim history of repression. That is why the Church cannot escape some measure of guilt for our contemporary nuclear fantasy. The Eucharist may yet, however, have the power to remind us that we are part of a humanity that carries that destructive archetype within us. Our symbols are fractured body and spilt blood:

> . . . one hesitates to imagine what kind of regime the IRA, the Baader-Meinhof gang or the Red Brigades would establish if they ever succeeded in achieving their objectives. 'In the name of the people' they would doubtless round up all 'enemies of society' and treat them with the same consideration as did Hitler, Stalin or Pol Pot. Repressed archetypal components tend to erupt in primitive destructive ways, primarily because they emerge in undifferentiated form from the unconscious . . .   (A. Stevens)[9]

The Christian Church should not forget that it celebrates the Eucharist 'in the name of the people', and not fail to heed the warning.

That raises a key question about what or who we do worship. Would I sacrifice my son, daughter, wife, lover or anything at the moment of sacrificial Eucharist? Am I celebrating success on the Stock Exchange, my child passing preparatory school entrance exams, a friend being made a bishop, a good night of sex, Arsenal winning in the 88th

minute? What do we worship and adore? This prayer of
Eucharist is about giving God his true worth and recognising
the idols and enemies which would destroy my humanity.
The clear structure of this prayer and its symbols, so simple
and profound, stop me worrying about who I am. It provides
a discipline within which I can break out and discover myself
in a fresh way. When the Host is finally raised I have a clue
in the midst of all my personal and collective pain to my final
stature as a person.

It should be obvious from my imaginary journey that I
regard the Eucharist as a great movement of symbol and
colour, choreography and drama. I believe that much worship
actually deprives people of the opportunity to experience
those heights and depths because it has stripped the liturgy
of movement. It has become static and people have become
frozen within it. I shall consider symbolism in chapter 5,
but we need to note here that the preparation of eucharistic
celebration needs much more care than is common in many
congregations.

I also want to note the contemporary move to make every
eucharist bear all the burdens of human belonging. We do
not recognise the difference between a cell, a congregation
and a cathedral. Too many congregations demand that they
are both cathedral and cell. The Eucharist can be used in a
multitude of ways. But we cannot expect the grandeur of
cathedral worship in a congregation of sixty with an electronic
organ. Nor can we demand the intimacy and warmth that
comes from belonging to a cell from the congregation. We
need to treat liturgical texts as resources to be drawn on
appropriately in different contexts with the maximum degree
of flexibility. At present ecclesiastical regulations lead to that
oppressive conformity to liturgical texts which is the death
knell of so much worship. Documents like the Anglican Alternative Service Book, and the equivalents in almost all the
other churches, can work like a strait jacket. They are our
most important resources but they should be used flexibly
and imaginatively. Pastoral criteria have not always been a
major factor in shaping their content. They need, therefore,
to be approached sceptically. I shall return to that theme
when dealing with sexist language (chapter 7) and with the
absence of confession in the funeral liturgies (chapter 6).

My imaginary journey was a spontaneous event which then required explanation. I did not construct it around certain psychological theories. As I struggled to explain it to myself I was struck again and again by what Jung called 'synchronicity'; by associations and connections in many places. I felt as if I were living at a particular depth of human feeling and that is why I risk sharing it in this book. I do not believe that it is either unique or perversely individual. The Christian Eucharist is the consummation of a process that has been developing in the human psyche for thousands of years. In order to grasp its significance it demanded a flow of imagination and vulnerability. Unless we allow our imagination to move between the actual reality and the unrealised ideal, how will we ever fully enter the depths of its mystery and really offer our sacrifice on the altar of the world?

1. Rowan Williams, *Resurrection* (DLT 1982), p. 108.
2. Ibid., p. 25.
3. Tissa Balasuriya, *The Eucharist and Human Liberation* (SCM 1977) p. 62.
4. Arthur Vogel, *Is the Last Supper Finished?* (New York 1968), p. 64.
5. Alan Ecclestone, *A Staircase for Silence* (DLT 1977), p. 81.
6. C. G. Jung, *Collected Works*, vol. 2: *Transformation Symbolism in the Mass* (Routledge 1958), p. 273.
7. Ibid., pp. 218–19.
8. Sebastian Moore, *The Crucified is No Stranger* (DLT 1977), Introduction, page x.
9. Anthony Stevens, *Archetype* (Routledge 1982), p. 122.

4

The Breaking Waters

... the use of water represents a purification of creation, a dying to that which is negative and destructive in the world ... (Lima text on *Baptism, Eucharist and Ministry*.)

This is the beginning of a dialogue between Diane, a single parent, and Mary, a Methodist minister:

DIANE: I've come to see if you'll do my baby.

MARY: Do your baby, Diane? Tell me more.

DIANE: Well, you see, I took him to this Church of England vicar up the road. He wanted to know if I believed in Jesus as my Saviour and who the godparents were to be . . . oh, he called them something like sponsors . . . and what did they believe and did they go to church regular . . . Christ, the kid ain't got a father let alone sponsors!

MARY: It sounds as if you're under a lot of pressure, Diane.

DIANE: You can say that again. You see, my mum insists that I get 'im done. Well, that's fine. I agree he ought to be done, but that vicar said we'd have to go at 9.30 in the morning . . . oh, I bet they're a really snotty crowd up there. I don't want to go and be looked down on.

MARY. Are you feeling a bit guilty about . . . what's his name?

DIANE: Oh, it's Jimmy . . . at least it will be when you've given 'im a name.

MARY: You say you agree with your mum that Jimmy should be baptised.

DIANE: Well, I think so. It's a sort of feeling right down inside me . . . (*She burst into tears*). Oh, God, it's all too much . . . I don't know how I'm going to cope . . . please,

please. I just want 'im done. I don't want all this trouble. Please do 'im . . . please.

(*Silence as Diane continues to cry.*)

MARY: It feels to me as though there is a great big struggle going on inside you. The struggle seems to overwhelm you.

DIANE (*still crying*):   Oh, I don't know what it is. The other night . . .

MARY: Uhm?

DIANE: The other night I just shook 'im . . . and shook 'im . . . then I thought I was looking into this dark hole . . .

MARY: That must have been really terrifying.

(*Diane continues to cry.*)

Baptism provides one of the surest tests of our readiness to allow pastoral criteria to determine our liturgical response. It is an area that is frequently fraught with pastoral difficulties. It also raises questions about the integrity of the Church's belief and practice. There is immense confusion in baptismal practice and theology among the different Christian denominations. But it is only today that Christians are beginning to comprehend again something of the significance of baptism for understanding what the grace of God might be about in terms of everyday living. Serious distortions in our understanding of baptism have acute pastoral repercussions. Geoffrey Lampe saw this all too clearly:

> Since baptism encompasses the whole Christian life, lack of clarity concerning the meaning of baptism leads to uncertainty all along the line . . . The more the baptised learn to see their whole life in the light of their baptism, the more does their life take on the pattern of life 'in Christ'. It is also of decisive importance to pastoral care to say to a troubled human being, 'You are baptised,' with all the assurance which this implies.[1]

The tension that I want to explore is between some basic human needs that lead people to ask for their children to be baptised and the Church's tradition about baptism. The pastoral question is how to do justice to the integrity of both. It may not always seem that human desires for baptism are an issue of integrity. The external social pressures from family and from an establishment society, superstition about the destiny of the child, may not at first sight seem like issues of integrity. Nevertheless, I shall argue that at more fundamental levels of personality there is an unconscious intent, part of the individuation process, which drives people towards the sacrament of baptism. I shall also want to argue that a dynamic understanding of sacrament can speak the good news of Jesus to that unconscious intent.

We are in difficulty in the contemporary Church because the sacramental life has become a captive of a rationalism, which is now almost played out. Some Christian traditions, reinforced by the attitudes of scientific materialism, have laid an emphasis on the necessity of certain *a priori* commitments or experiences for the reception of the sacraments. The primary responsibility rests on the worthiness or commitment of whoever wants to take part. When people like Diane get caught up into that, it induces guilt and despair. Her encounter with the Church of England vicar simply reminded her of her failure, confusion and hesitant faith. It has to be said that this is a long way from Christian orthodoxy. Sacraments are events, communally celebrated, in which the material universe becomes the means for the action of God. Christian theology understands God to be the actor and therefore sacramental life is not dependent upon how good or holy or believing we are. The genius of a sacrament is to liberate us from the tyranny of being religious.

In 1982 the group responsible for the Christian presence at that strange bazaar of the human spirit, the Festival of Mind, Body and Spirit, took as its theme 'By Water and the Word'. The stand was dominated by a huge icon of 'The Baptism of Jesus'. During the week those staffing the stand gave away cups of cold water. At no point did Olympia, the conference hall in London, become hot during that week, but the demand for cups of cold water was immense. The gift of water led to numerous conversations about hope and love. That illustrates for me something of the symbolic power of water.

In many of the world's traditions, water is linked to the deep-down unconscious forces of life. It is an image of primal matter, something of basic significance for the bearing of life.

At birth the waters have to break for the child to be born. To St John Chrysostom it symbolised that universal potentiality signifying both death and regeneration: 'It represents death and interment, life and resurrection . . . When we plunge our head beneath water, as in a sepulchre, the old man becomes completely immersed and buried. When we leave the water, the new man suddenly appears . . .'[2] Water, like most symbols, is ambiguous because it contains the contradictions of destruction and creation. Water is a symbol of struggle that goes on in the psychic depths of people.

Some of that struggle can be discovered in ordinary domestic situations. Children ask fundamental questions about existence when they are in the bath. Hydrotherapy is commonly used in the treatment of disturbed and handicapped people. Water is vital for existence. In meditation I experience a still pool of water within myself.

Baptism, I want to suggest, touches this level of being. It is unconscious, irrational, emotive and affective. It carries some of the basic anxieties of living with it. Because water is both a creative and destructive force, it puts human beings in touch with both sides of themselves. Requests for baptism may reflect this level of pastoral need. We cannot assume that people are able to put into words, let alone the words of cerebral Christianity, these unconscious needs. But it may be these deep, irrational and unconscious forces that lead many people to ask for Christian baptism. On the whole the Churches respond to this situation in the classic Western manner. They produce cerebral and intellectual approaches to the sacrament and expect people to express their belief in words. But there is a strangeness about human experience that cannot always be expressed in that way. It is not possible to account for the continuing desire for baptism simply in terms of rational Christian faith. We are dealing with a more archaic phenomenon, which Christian symbolism has illuminated in past centuries:

> But water is earthy and tangible, it is also the fluid of the instinct-driven body, blood and the flowing of blood, the odour of the beast, carnally heavy with passion. The unconscious is the psyche that reaches down from the mentally

and morally lucid consciousness into the nervous system
that for ages has been known as the 'sympathetic' . . .
(C. G. Jung)[3]

That level of being demands a pastoral response that I can
only call 'reverential'. Attempting to respond to it by intellectual answers will usually only deepen the resistance and make
the demands for baptism even more strident.

This is the beginning of what I mean by the unconscious
intent of those who seek baptism. Clergy who seek to frustrate
that intent must expect to meet with some resistance. That
does not mean that I am advocating baptism without
discrimination. It does mean that I am again suggesting that
the resistance is a pastoral opportunity. We mask and avoid
those elements of human experience, like the death-and-life
struggle, which most disconcert us. There is something in the
symbol of water that both threatens and promises. Pastors
have to take hold of that ambiguity and use it creatively.
Even Calvin acknowledged that it was by 'earthly elements'[4]
that God leads us to himself.

I would like to stay with that theme of the creative and
destructive forces within people. The waters of baptism into
which Jesus entered were the dwelling place of the monsters
that threatened human life. In the great Orthodox mosaics
of Creation and Baptism, Jesus is the one who tramples down
the monsters. The water are, therefore, part of that system of
violence and destruction, with the consequences of guilt and
fear, into which human beings are drawn. Part of that system
of violence and destruction is what I want to call the ambiguity of parenthood. The Church has so idealised the family
that it may be very difficult indeed for some Christians to
hear what I now want to say. Nevertheless my own experience
as a father and as a confessor leaves me in no doubt that
there is truth in it. In the matter of the family, Church and
society are in collusion. TV commercials, reinforced by the
traditional representations of Madonna and Child, represent
a view of the relationship of parents to children which is
inconsistent with reality. Numerous parents, even those with
devout faith, know that in the darkness of the night it is
possible to be driven right to the edge of the abyss of violence
with small children. Even in the day mothers, and some

fathers, sit by small children with songs of silent pain. Yet there is a massive collusion in Western society against honest talking about the ambiguity of parenthood. The truth is that in many families, mothers and fathers slide down the razor-blade edge between violence and love. Many live a hair's breadth away from being a child batterer. The Church makes no contribution to society's health by colluding with a mystique that the family does not share in this web of systemic violence. The family is part of it and the risk of violence grows even greater as social cohesiveness breaks down and human isolation increases. Diane knew something about this ambiguity of parenthood and was beginning to express it at the end of the dialogue.

Among all the social pressures and etiquettes which drive people to desire baptism for their children, pastors should expect to discover some who share in this web of violence. In fact, I would challenge the Church to rediscover its historic sense of how people shield themselves against this self-know-ledge. I doubt if there are many parents who do not experience feelings of violence in some way. It may be precisely that ambiguous mix of violence and love that causes the desire for baptism in the first place.

Over that systemic violence, the baptism of Jesus opens up a new vision. Part of its meaning is that you are not hated or abandoned in the isolation of death and violence but are the recipient of a new name and identity:

> We who have made God's love contingent on human good-ness, human response, human feelings, and human under-standing need to hear baptism's word of comfort to those in our midst who despair over who they are and to whom they belong. We have clouded our proclamation of faith with talk about who we ought to be when we should have taken our cue from baptism and spoken more of who by God's grace, we are.   (W. H. Willimon)[5]

The request for baptism will sometimes reveal other pastoral needs. In Diane's case, there seemed to be an unresolved issue about being a single parent as well as problems about her relationship with her own mother. The latter had become centred in the question of Jimmy's baptism. People have a need to be restored to a community because they feel unacceptable or isolated. Requests for baptism can often cloak pastoral needs in the family presenting the child. In any baptismal ritual there could be an equal need for Diane to be restored to her own baptismal status as someone in receipt of the grace of God. In that sense baptism is both a once-for-all event and a continuing characteristic of Christian living. Even if we discriminate about who should or should not be baptised, we should remember that all cases need to be treated with reverence. They reflect a pastoral need. The ministry of discerning those needs is one of the skills of the true pastor. You can't say No and claim that God in Jesus died for the whole of humanity.

The colossal forces symbolised by the universal threat of nuclear conflict increasingly leave people feeling powerless and unable to share in social responsibility. One serious consequence of that is the erosion of any sense of identity. People feel 'done to' if they feel involved at all. It seems almost pointless even to ask the question, 'Who am I?' Baptism certainly raises the question because it is a sacrament about identity and value. It is the ordination of the people of God. God makes himself available to us through visible means, through which we know ourselves to be valued and loved. There is absolutely nothing we can do about it. Baptism finally saves us from the perverse human tyranny of being good. Anyone who counsels people knows that that tyranny wreaks havoc in people as they try not only to live up to unrealistic parental expectations but also to live down their sense of failure and impotence. When baptism is offered it is in terms of a new identity, which is not dependent on such deceptive illusions. This sense of personal value given freely by God is in the end the foundation of all social and political responsibility: baptism is also 'done to' me but it liberates me for responsible action in the face of the holocaust. 'He has delivered us from the dominion of darkness and transferred us to the kingdom of his beloved Son, in whom we have redemption, the forgiveness of sins' (Colossians 1:13–14, RSV). Our fundamental value as people rests in the grace of God alone.

In this sense baptism meets another of what Abraham Maslow called 'the hierarchy of basic needs'. Through it we find a home and a place to belong. For all its manifest failings, the Church is the place where the new system of relationships is to be recognised and appropriated. The identity given in baptism is both a sense of individual value and a life lived in mutuality and forgiveness. Jesus reveals human life as it really is: the Church is the continuation of that process. The baptismal community is always a living reminder that the weak and the vulnerable belong together with the adult and the strong. Baptism is also about cherishing each other in the social and political realms. The Church offers the world a vision of a community that is not afraid to offer positive discrimination to the marginal, the weak and the poor. The glory of Jesus, the Gospel of John reminds us, is judgement to the strong and the powerful who rely upon a glory that has not been purified by the moral imagination. Pope Callistus insisted during his reign that slaves should bring the offering of water in the sacraments: he underlined their worth in the only offering they could make.

If baptism is Easter made visible, then it is a passover event marking a movement from one state to another. In the language of anthropology, it is a *rite de passage*. In almost all of the world's rituals, which effect a change in the status of a person, there are three stages: separation, transition and incorporation. Arnold Van Gennep, in his classic study *The Rites of Passage*, says of Christian baptism:

> Baptism has not often been regarded as a lustration, a purging and purifying rite, i.e. a final rite of separation from the previous world, whether it be a secular world or one that is actually impure. This rite must be evaluated with care, however, for it may also signify incorporation when it is performed with consecrated rather than with ordinary water. In that case the person baptised not only loses an attribute but also gains one.[6]

The dialogue between Diane and Mary at the opening of this chapter begins to illustrate that movement in a rather vivid way. Diane was concerned that her son should begin a new life; she was also concerned that he would become part of a community. She was attempting to find her way. The extraordinary factor in Diane's case is that she too needs to make the baptismal transition. Although in one sense baptism is a once-for-all-event, the renewal of baptismal promises also helps us to go on feeling this sense of belonging. In this sense the Church's rituals continue to exercise a vital pastoral function within the community.

That raises an important issue about baptism. Baptism must be understood as an act of grace by Christ within the Church. The New Testament evidence is clear at this point: the responsibility and the resources for baptism are given to the Church (see Matthew 28:18–19; Acts 8:12–13). The Church's task is not to shift that responsibility onto the backs of those whom we are supposed to initiate into the Kingdom of God. In most arguments about infant baptism, the responsibility of the Church as the agent of the Kingdom is ignored. Instead we become obsessed with the belief credentials or conversion experiences of those who ask for baptism. I am not denying that a response of faith is required; but I am arguing that the burden of responsibility lies with the baptisers who are to demonstrate the anarchic grace of God. When we lay the burden on the parents or on the person desiring baptism, we are not being pastoral. We are caught in a downward spiral of not depending on grace alone. It is, of course, disturbing to a Church which is obsessed with pecking orders and status to suggest that status is given rather than earned. But that is the reality of baptism. The ecumenical statement on baptism produced by the major world Churches, the Lima document on *Baptism, Eucharist and Ministry*, makes it clear that this is what baptism is about:

> Baptism initiates the reality of the new life given in the midst of the present world. It gives participation in the Holy Spirit. It is a sign of the Kingdom of God and of the life of the world to come. Through the gifts of faith, hope and love, baptism has a dynamic which embraces the whole of life . . .[7]

Note how the words 'gift' and 'given' echo through that statement.

If the responsibility for baptism clearly rests on both pastoral and theological grounds with the Christian community, there are some implications for its practice. On both grounds, private baptism is a contradiction in terms, for if baptismal faith is about living together in reciprocity, then that must be expressed in the ritual. If it is to be true to its pastoral, anthropological, theological and psychological derivations, it must be a communal event. The identity given in baptism is forever dependent on the life of the Christian community, and gives us a glimpse of something infinitely greater: ' . . . the use of water . . . signifies the continuity between the old and new creation, thus revealing the significance of baptism not only for human beings but also for the whole cosmos' (Lima document).[8] Baptism should therefore take place within the worship of the whole congregation. Theological arguments for that have often been made, and pastoral concerns amplify that conviction.

One of the ways to do that would be to revive the notion that Lent is a time of preparation for baptism, and that Holy Saturday is the great festival of baptism. If baptism is Easter made visible, that is the time for baptism to be practised fully. The much greater use of water, oil, candles, laying on of hands, darkness and light, and the renewal of vows all gives reality to what I have called the unconscious intent. Those symbols are powerful enough to contain the ambiguous oppositions within people. There is an urgent pastoral, as well as theological, case to be made for restoring baptism to the Church's liturgical focus, the great Easter vigil and baptismal celebration. Many people need help today in the rituals of endings and new beginnings. As someone, who has been divorced, I know that we need rituals to free us from domination by our past failures and to reincorporate us in the new humanity of Christ. I believe that the renewal of baptism vows is just such a pastoral opportunity.

If there is to be rigour in the question of baptism, the rigour should lie in the preparation for baptism rather than in a rigid policy of refusing it. I believe that this is also good pastoral and evangelical practice. There is some evidence in surveys undertaken in south London that loving attention given to people at major turning points in their lives can actually lead to active faith in Christ.[9] This suggests that baptismal preparation may be one key to active Christian discipleship. The problem with a lot of baptismal catechesis is that it is based on a notion of education: that is, the transmission of knowledge from one party to another. Those 'in the know' pass it on to those who don't know. That assumes a model of knowledge which is anti-baptismal because it is education based on power. (See also chapter 2.)

I would like to propose a different model, which I believe is more consistent with what the baptismal community is like. If it is a community where the vulnerable and strong cherish each other, then learning comes by reflection, relating a growing familiarity with the Christian tradition to the activities of everyday living. It is because people are often not encouraged by the Church to integrate their life experience with the experience of God that 'the penny does not drop'. We need to remember too, that we are learning in a context today where there is very little understanding of Christian belief. Many young parents, the products of post-war education, know almost nothing about Christian faith. The Church left to the state education system the responsibility for Christian nurture and it is paying a terrible price for the abandonment of its responsibility.

Here is a skeleton outline for baptismal preparation, which tries to take seriously both the integrity of human experience and the integrity of the Gospel of God. Each of the areas could provide material for one or more sessions:

(a) An explanation of the significance of water: what meanings does it have? What do people associate with it? Perhaps people could be encouraged to go on a fantasy journey (see chapter 3) along a river by the sea, around a lake. Biblical material: Exodus 14:15–31; Mark 4:35–41; Luke 3:19–20.

(b) 'Everything is all right'? When a child screams in the middle of the night and a parent gives this assurance are they lying or telling the truth? Where do we get our value from? Who am I? What do we want our child to be? Biblical material: Romans 6:3–11; Ephesians 2:7–10.

(c) Do parents experience violence in themselves? Or towards their children? What do they feel about violence to children? Are there parts of themselves or their lives they would want to be separated from? How do they feel we collude with a violent world and about their feelings of powerlessness in it? Biblical material: 1 Peter 3:18–22; Colossians 1:12–14.

(d) What does 'home' mean? Do words like 'belonging' and 'together' have important meanings? What are they? What does 'finding a home' imply? Biblical material: Ephesians 3:14–21; Luke 8:19–21.

(e) What kind of community do I want to belong to? Locally? Nationally? Internationally? What kind of world do we want for our children? If God has no grandchildren, what kind of community would he want? Do we have a part in creating the future together? Biblical material; Galatians 3:27–9; Ephesians 2:13–22.

(f) What would you be prepared to sacrifice for your child? What do we really believe in? What do you have faith in? Would you be prepared to die for anything? Biblical material: John 3:4–8; Colossians 2:12–15.

Many clergy will say that this material is too rigorous for baptismal preparation. I am arguing that rigour is a proper respect for the integrity of human experience and the integrity of the gospel. There is an urgent need for baptism to be restored to the centre of Christian experience and worship. It addresses in a narcissistic age some of the most fundamental questions of identity and value in our corrupt Western society. It is a proper meeting place for pastoral reverence and evangelistic integrity.

Before ending this chapter I shall make three further points. The first is about the pastoral needs of children in worship. Post-baptismal catechesis is just as important as pre-baptismal preparation. It cannot be said too strongly that children have very rich resources of imagination. Their natural capacity for this and the symbolic world they inhabit makes it possible for them to participate fully in worship. The worshipping community will need to find a proper rhythm between the specific needs of children being met and their participation in the worship of the wider community. It will not always be easy to find that rhythm because of the complex needs that all bring to worship. But much can be achieved by, for example, developing the ministry of the word in the Eucharist at a time when different groups within the congregation work at themes at their own level and in their own ways. Much more work could be done in preparing educational material for a wide range of age groups. This is not to underestimate the value and importance of preaching, which I value very highly and will deal with in chapter 8. But I am suggesting that throughout our lives we learn in a whole variety of ways and these should be reflected in liturgy. Much of our ritual is an insult to the sensitivity and imagination of children. In many churches, children are not even recognised as part of the baptismal Easter community. Their activities, if they happen at all, take place at a time different from the main liturgy. We need to rediscover Christian nurture from the cradle to the grave. It is legitimate to argue that too much of the Church's resources has been put into the nurture of children. But that does not mean that we can ignore the pastoral needs of children for belonging.

The second point is about the controversial issue of confirmation. I doubt if there is any serious theological argument for the rite of confirmation at all. Baptism by its very nature leads to the eucharistic sharing of Christ's body and blood. The rite of confirmation is a question mark over the significance of baptism; it questions its final status. My difficulty is that confirmation may make quite good pastoral sense because it enables young people to make an important transition. It is the theological equivalent to puberty and may make a significant contribution to the health of the community. It is an initiation rite that makes possible a move towards greater maturity. In a society that is deprived of initiation rites, the Church may be playing an important function in providing a rite that works for females as well as males. Anthony Stevens draws attention to the devastating consequences of a society without initiation rites:

. . . the Self actually anticipates that some form of initiation procedure will be vested in the culture. If this is so, then it is reasonable to assume that societies which provide no puberty rites will produce a large population of males in whom the masculine principle is partially actualised.

Certainly, this would seem to be the case in contemporary Western society.[10]

I leave the paradox thus: how can a theological contradiction also be a pastoral necessity?

My third point relates to the question of services for the blessing of children, which some churches suggest for those who are not regular worshippers. Most of the major Churches have discovered alternatives to baptism. These arose partly out of a concern that baptism should not be indiscriminately administered and partly out of respect for the integrity of parents in a post-Christian age. Pastoral care will always be concerned with integrity and nobody would, I hope, regard it as good pastoral practice for people to make dishonest vows. Nevertheless, I have an anxiety that these para-liturgies do not always meet the need expressed, simply because they are not capable of responding to the unconscious intent I discussed earlier. Some way has to be found of making the Christian resources available to those who cannot with honesty share the significance of the symbols offered. But my doubt remains: I suspect that these para-liturgies are often means of laying the burden of proof on the recipients rather than on the baptising community. A really rigorous catechesis, which enabled people to connect their everyday human experience with the gift of grace, might be a far more satisfactory way ahead in many cases. The Church is meant to be a moment of disclosure about Jesus!

Let us return to Diane and Mary. We were beginning to catch a glimpse of the chaos inside Diane. She sensed that her son shared in that chaos, and she was looking for a symbol which would bring order out of this inner chaos and the conflicts of her life. That symbol was to touch the depths of her life, releasing the energy that would lead her and her son into a new world. She looked for it in the primal Christian sacrament of baptism. In her pilgrimage, she looked for the assurance that her mistakes were not the final word about her. She was seeking a reconciliation between all that she dreaded about herself and her world and a universal vision. She found it finally in the breaking of the waters. Her son has heard the words: 'You have a meaning which it will take the rest of your life to unravel.'

So Mary did baptise Jimmy. Reflecting on the experience afterwards, she had no doubt that it was a right action. It had helped her to understand the grace of God much more. She spent a lot of time with Diane and still wonders if the renewal of her baptismal promises was adequate for her need. But both Diane and Jimmy are part of a living Christian community and in that Diane is finding healing and has passed over from despair to hope. When the waters break, the new pass-over begins!

1. G. W. H. Lampe and D. M. Paton, *One Lord, One Baptism* (SCM 1960), p. 70.
2. St John Chrysostom, *Homil. in Joh.*, xxv, 2.
3. C. G. Jung, *Collected Works*, vol. 9 (Routledge 1959), part 1, p. 19.
4. J. Calvin, *Institutes of the Christian Religion*, IV 14 3 (Westminster Press 1960), ii, 1278.
5. W. H. Willimon, *Worship as Pastoral Care* (Abingdon 1979), p. 160.
6. A. Van Gennep, *The Rites of Passage* (Routledge), p. 63.
7. World Council of Churches, *Baptism, Eucharist and Ministry* (Faith and Order Paper no. 111, 1982), p. 3.
8. Ibid., p. 7.
9. Two surveys were undertaken in the Anglican deaneries of Wandsworth and Merton in south London to discover the routes by which new Christians had come to active faith. They both revealed that the largest group (in each case over 50 per cent) had come to faith through ministry given at a major turning point, e.g. the birth of a child, bereavement, divorce, etc. Events like evangelistic campaigns or special services were quite insignificant compared with that group.
10. Anthony Stevens, *Archetype* (Routledge, 1982), p. 158.

5

Opening Gates of Vision

Between the altar and the faithful from year to year a moat was widening, filled with dead words.   (ALEJO CARPENTIER)

A woman lay dying in a London hospice. During the last week of her life she began to draw a story. It was a story about a small boy and a dragon. Day after day the boy and the dragon battled on the pages of her notebook. The day after she died the senior nurse found, on the last page of the notebook, the small boy and the dragon standing hand in hand. Both were smiling.

If worship is about humanity 'in its wholeness wholly attending' (D. H. Lawrence), we cannot avoid the issue of symbolism in worship. Every human life needs a coherent symbolic system. Much of the argument of this book rests on the view that the unconscious is a reality and that a symbolic structure is necessary for human life to flourish. If ritual is to become an environment within which people grow, it will need to be symbolic and mythological, i.e. symbols will be related to each other in a coherent way. The woman in the hospice needed to sort out complex emotions so that they were not only comprehensible to her but also communicable to others. She used a symbolic construction to deal with the ultimate issue of life, death. That provides us with an analogy of how ritual works in relation to the complex pastoral needs of people.

This may not be readily understood in the contemporary Church. It has been slowly reducing ritual to linguistic codes. Get the words right and all will be well. It is already clear that things are far from well. The anthropologist, Mary Douglas, reflects on liturgical reforms in the Roman Catholic Church and reaches the conclusion:

> . . . we have seen that those who are responsible for ecclesiastical decisions are only too likely to have been made, by the manner of their education, insensitive to non-verbal signals and dull to their meaning. This is central to the difficulties of Christianity today. It is as if the liturgical signal boxes were manned by colour-blind signalmen.[1]

The development of symbolic boundaries is one of the ways in which order is brought into the chaos that threatens life. Those symbols make it possible for us to relate to each other in new ways and attune us to the ultimate meaning of life. The stripping down of ritual and liturgy into ethical language does not really promote the health of a person on their deathbed. There is no possibility of justification by good works then! Social responsibility is no substitute for symbols through which we relate to each other. In fact the renewed emphasis on social ethics and public responsibility is likely to be defeated in the absence of adequate symbolic systems. People are deprived of precisely those resources they need for making an adequate ethical response.

There is a real moral and human issue here. If the Church wants Christians to engage in socio-political action, then it has a responsibility to provide those resources that make that possible. It is not caring to lay huge ethical responsibilities on individuals without providing an adequate symbolic framework with which to respond to those responsibilities. Those who most despise symbolism in worship must recognise that they are frustrating the unconscious intent in people. The longing to communicate without words has its roots in the basic relationship of human life: 'However gratifying it is in later life to express thoughts and feelings to a congenial person, there remains an unsatisfied longing for an understanding without words – ultimately for the earliest relation with the mother' (Melanie Klein).[2]

We must, nevertheless, recognise that there is a problem. The search for this conscious freedom, that the woman in the hospice realised, is frustrated in contemporary Western society. A significant shift has taken place. Instead of seeking to maintain the integrity of the community we place the development and the protection of the individual at the centre of our concern. This has important consequences, one of which is the placing of economic exchange at the centre of our world of meanings. Another consequence is that it perpetuates the emergence of the 'inner directed character' (see chapter 1). Symbols and myths are no longer dominant features of key areas of life, although very powerful symbols of human powerlessness persist on cinema screens: the 'Towering Inferno' is a powerful symbol of the repressed terror of being human and helpless, but there may be virtue in that powerlessness. If people in the rich North can admit that they are no longer the masters of the world, a new dialogue can start with those who value the archaic and symbolic understandings of community. Christian ritual may yet have a part to play in helping us deal with the anxiety of powerlessness in the face of impending chaos:

> The people of the Inner City are not voyeurs looking in on life before passing on . . . they tell of a God whose symbols various as they are about the realities of life – babies wanted and unwanted; flowers sharp with colour in the morning fading as the day grows old; the open hand (not of the 'beggar' or the 'stranger' – those are the words of the aliens) of the sister or the brother who shares with everyone the rights and dignity of being human and who needs also to share in the otherwise unequal distribution of the world's resources.   (Don Pickard)[3]

Symbols open up people living with limited freedom to a world in which a new kind of conscious freedom may be claimed.

The anthropologist Sherry Ortner, in exploring the pastoral significance of symbols in liturgy, distinguishes between 'elaborating' and 'summarising' symbols.[4] 'Elaborating' symbols are the means by which we sort out our undifferentiated, and often confusing, mass of feelings and ideas in order to make sense of a chaotic world. Water is an elaborating symbol. 'Summarising' symbols sum up in a powerful way what a whole system of belief means. The Christian crucifix or empty cross would be one such symbol. It draws together a complex system of convictions in a way which unifies them and focusses commitment and faith in a way that leads to either ethical choice or creative action. The distinction between 'elaborating' and 'summarising' symbols is important, because it enriches the range of understanding symbol. Most of the current writing about the use of symbol in Christian ritual deals only with 'summarising' symbols. An exploration of 'elaborating' symbols helps us tease out the archaic meaning of Christian symbols in contemporary life. Symbols are not only for interpreting. They exist to puzzle us out.

We depend upon symbols because of our sensitivity to experiences with which we may be unable to cope. Those experiences are about anxieties at the boundaries of life. The first, and perhaps most obvious, of those anxieties is that of suffering; it threatens our sense of order and known patterns of living. Most hospital patients are familiar with the rapid transition from a wide cone of living to the narrow cone of the hospital bed. There is a diminishment in the scale of living, and this can be paralleled by an emotional one. If suffering is severe, it almost always raises problems of meaning and significance. The pastoral problem is about how to support others in their suffering while taking serious account of their own symbolic world. Here is a case study to illustrate what I mean.

A woman had been in labour for a very long time and the birth was proving very difficult. She asked to see a chaplain. The chaplaincy was called, and the Free Church chaplain who was on duty came. He was met at the door of the labour room by the doctor and the nurse who remarked cynically, 'Well, nothing else is working so we may as well try prayer.'

The chaplain was ushered in, and after a brief talk he prayed: 'Father we ask that your loving presence be felt in a very real way by this your child as she struggles in the pangs of her own child's birth. We're grateful that you are with us wherever life's circumstances may take us; that no matter what happens to us, we have your promise that you'll never leave us comfortless either now or forevermore. We pray this . . .' Twenty minutes later the woman gave birth to a son.[5]

The chaplain had understood that the woman was on a boundary of anxiety and needed someone around who symbolised some ultimate purpose within which she could relax. The chaplain was able to express that in his prayer, and so enabled her to relax and have the baby. He was able to keep his own integrity by recognising that he was using a broken symbol that was able to connect with her own symbolic values. He was a priest holding her in the presence of God through a sacred symbol.

At the boundary of suffering, the reworking of the symbol of the cross remains powerful. The pastoral dilemma for numerous people is as much how to suffer as why they are suffering. Hans Ruedi-Weber has studied the cross in many cultures across the world. He reflects on both the limitations of the symbol and its power:

> All Christian art can only point to the true image of God which became manifest in Jesus Christ not least when he was nailed on the cross. Yet there is a more existential way of making that image visible – by ourselves being transfigured into this 'icon' of God which appeared in Christ . . .[6]

The cross is a way of affirming the inescapability of pain and suffering. At the same time it denies that chaos is the end of living. The dragon and the child spoke of that same paradox to the woman dying in the hospice. They became a metaphor of meaning because they were a way of bringing order to existence and investing it with significance.

The second radical challenge to the intelligibility of the world is at the boundary of meaning and human responsibility. Despite the immense strides in scientific discovery there remains a boundary where problems remain because the more unmanageable dimensions of human skill lead to disquiet. Things cry out for human explanation but we are left with a deep disquiet that no explanation is possible. This is most powerfully experienced in the face of nuclear fission, the DNA vortex and genetic engineering. There is an amazing ambiguity about much of the universe, which leaves us perplexed and perhaps estranged. Many attempts at explaining such a cosmos have developed out of experiences of exile and estrangement. The Creation myths in the book of Genesis are the products of struggles to give symbolic form to experiences of oppression, exile and restoration. The attempt to secure a social identity and the meaning of the world belonged together.

The symbolic myths of universal creation are attempts to shape that chaotic world of violation and identity. Perhaps one of the urgent tasks facing the Church is the creation of a new symbolic world which will take account of scientific discovery, of all the ways the empirical world has been mapped, and the nature of the Christian God. A doctrinal crisis has been brewing in the Anglican Church for some time about the omnipotence of God. The struggle to understand God afresh is part of the response required in the face of chaotic threats to humanity and to the very existence of the universe. Mircea Eliade sets the historical context for that monumental task:

> It shows up very clearly a specific condition of man in the cosmos – what we may call 'the nostalgia for Paradise'. I mean by this the desire to be always effortlessly, at the heart of the world, of reality, of the sacred, and briefly, to transcend, by natural means, the human condition and regain a divine state of affairs . . .[7]

Christianity focussed on Jesus has some radical questions to ask about 'the nostalgia for Paradise', but the Church cannot avoid the question that Eliade raises about our symbolic grasp of the cosmos in which we live.

The third boundary, which perplexes people, is that between good and evil. There is an acute problem today: we have the symbolic resources in the Judaeo-Christian tradition for a rigorous estimate of justice and oppression, but are we able to translate those resources into adequate ethical criteria to govern our actions? I have been involved for nearly twenty years, through the World Development Movement and Christian Aid, in the struggle for a new international economic order. I am struck at how easy it is for people to run out of steam in that struggle. I think that sense of moral impotence is often accounted for by the lack of a symbolic framework. The principles and symbols which constitute the moral order are often difficult to grasp in the face of the enigmas and inexplicable pain of injustice. When justice seems like a mirage, we need our sense of hope renewed and our confidence in the providence of God confirmed. When there

appears to be no rational or moral coherence, another kind
of response is demanded: we need the image of a genuine
order in the world which contains its paradoxes, puzzles and
ambiguities.

There is an urgent need within the Church for a renewed
catholicism which will maintain a sense of wholeness. That
wholeness is not going to develop from churches becoming
sects but out of a renewed vision of those great symbols which
are latent in every person and which are celebrated in the
cosmic and metaphysical dramas of humanity. The need is
for a wholeness which takes serious account of the tragic irony
of evil, enabling us to live with the suffering and ambiguities
of the world. The worship of the Church needs that richness
of symbol because through it we can recognise the battle
between good and evil and begin to transcend it. There is a
tendency for liturgical commissions of all traditions to be
over-concerned with the right forms of words. We need, what
Fitzjames Stephen calls, 'someone who is so inspired as to set
to music the tune which is haunting millions of ears'.[8] The
cerebral ethos of the Church of England is unlikely to produce
such a person: that ethos is creating a sterile liturgy. So from
where can we expect such a person? If one of the symbolic
functions today is to reflect 'a global village', perhaps the
salvation of British liturgy may yet come from one of those
whom we oppressed in order to grow rich and satisfy our
missionary fervour. Almost every Christian tradition has
world-wide contacts, and partnership in mission is becoming
increasingly accepted as the norm. Christians from many
parts of the Third World have a great deal to teach us about
worship within this developing partnership.

The symbolic sterility in much Anglican worship is often
further perpetuated by the growing disuse of the Old Testament in its liturgy. Although the Alternative Service Book
has gone a little way to restoring its use, the verbal ritual of
Mattins and Evensong did at least regularly remind worshippers that God is a God of justice. Even in the suffocating self-
righteousness of some of the Psalms there is the constant
reminder that everyday living is the forum for acts of justice
and truth. We know that the righteous do not prosper, even
if some people do still look to such religious precepts for the
preservation of their particular values. The rhythmical recital

of the Psalms enabled people who heard their truth to recognise that the expression of real passion in the face of injustice was a proper Christian responsibility. They provided a symbolic framework for denying that the irrationality of evil and the triumph of injustice are final and irrevocable realities. The Psalms are a proclamation that life is not absurd. Their demise in much Christian ritual is an impoverishment of the human psyche. We are being slowly starved by liturgical innovation of adequate emotional and symbolic forms with which to stand on the boundary between good and evil. This leaves numerous people, confronted with the possibility of nuclear catastrophe, with the uncomfortable suspicion that there is no genuine moral order to the world after all.

It is through rituals, however simple and repetitious, that order and meaning are communicated. Symbolic forms fuse together the world as it is actually experienced with the world as imagined when the conflict of good and evil is resolved. In ritual we live through this symbolic fusion of our view of the world and a way of seeing all political, social, emotional and physical phenomena in a new light. As a university chaplain I had the immense privilege of living close to many young people who lived at the boundaries of doubt and faith. With them I had to learn that ritual was a way of making Christian concepts truthful. Many of those people had serious doubts about both the expression and the content of Christian faith. The liturgical texts and prayers were difficult for them because they did not immediately connect with the concrete and social circumstances of everyday living. They made me realise that liturgical renewal cannot be only about translating into the vernacular, simplifying the ritual, rewriting the texts. Ritual had to cohere with their moral vision. It had to be a dynamic process, a symbolisation process, in which they took their human experience, lived in the context of the historical and political evolution of the world, and brought that into contact with the Christian tradition. It was often, and still is, for many a problematical relationship. But, if liturgy and mission are to renew each other, opportunities must exist for the integration of our moral involvement and liturgical expression.

This interplay between liturgy and ethical involvement in the world is what I call the process of symbolisation. In that

interplay we need a decade of liturgical experiment in which
people are given the freedom to explore their aspirations to
be part of the Kingdom of God in relation to the symbols
and myths of the Christian tradition. Too much experimental
liturgy is based on the notion of worship as performance; I
suffered all too often as a university chaplain from being a
passive observer. The process of symbolisation presupposes
that everyone is a participant in the liturgical celebration of
the Kingdom of God. We are not in the business of producing
liturgical 'products'. The ritual must provide an opportunity
for all to express their aspirations in a coherent way. In some
American research into a group of young people developing
new liturgical forms, two major conclusions emerged:

> There was an obvious concern for concrete life, facts, situ-
> ations, people and the world and for the collection of infor-
> mation about Society, along with involvement in social
> needs, the development of solidarity, and care for people.
>
> There was a consciously expressed intention to celebrate
> the Eucharist together and to form a community that seri-
> ously reflected together and wanted to deepen the experi-
> ence of the uniqueness of the Christian faith.[9]

At every stage of life the search for conscious freedom is basic:
the process of symbolisation aids that search. Religious belief,
experienced symbolically in ritual, bursts open the everyday
world. Symbolism has what Mircea Eliade calls a 'porous-
ness'; it opens us up to other possibilities.

Let us look further at 'focussing' or 'summarising' symbols.
I was discussing with a Roman Catholic friend her change
from the Presbyterian Church. I asked about her symbolic
memories of her Presbyterian upbringing. 'Huh,' she
commented, 'there was only one. The huge collection plate
set right in the middle of the holy table!' Her further, unre-
peatable comments, suggested that it had not been an
adequate symbol to express the ambiguities of living in the
post-Hiroshima age. The same problem is explored in a novel
by the Jewish author, Chaim Potok. In *My Name is Asher Lev*,
the central character, Asher, struggles to make sense of his
experience, both collective and personal, unconscious and

conscious, inside the boundaries of contemporary Jewish ritual. He cannot deal with the ambiguities of contemporary New York within those limits. He is an artist and communicates new meaning through what for him is a scandalous symbol. His painting is named 'Brooklyn Crucifixion I and II':

> And it was then that it came, though I think it had been coming for a long time and I had been choking it and hoping it would die. But it does not die. It kills you first. I knew there would be no other way to do it. No one says you have to paint ultimate anguish and torment. But if you are driven to paint it, you have no other way . . . an observant Jew working on a crucifixion because there was no aesthetic mold in his own religious tradition into which he could pour a painting of ultimate anguish and torment.[10]

There is a radical understanding of the power of the 'summarising' symbol: it breaks through the boundaries of the past and becomes a focus for containing the agonising paradoxes and contradictions of being human. In that sense it is a new event.

Liturgy will be powerful when it breaks open the symbols of the Christian tradition in the same way. Many of those symbols are disturbed in their form: broken bread, poured oil, breaking waters, spilt wine. Anyone who has tried to be with someone who is wounded or perplexed knows that it is not long before contradictions show up. The struggle between love and hate, dependence and autonomy, lovability and self-loathing, loss and discovery and numerous other conflicts are all characteristics of the search to be more human. The power of symbol is that it can contain those opposites in ways that make for health and maturity. The dove, for example, so often a symbol of peace is a very violent bird. Liturgy is a system of relating those symbols together and a means through which we can begin to make sense of some of those contradictions. The problem with a lot of Christian worship is that it can repress one set of opposites in favour of another. One consequence of that is the frigid goodness which can be found in so many British congregations. I remember a priest exploding after a major anniversary celebration: 'I'd banish servers if I was given a chance . . . where the hell do they leave their humanity . . . at home in bed?' We parade our frigid goodness because the Church so often refuses that symbolic framework which could resolve our human contradictions. That is a further reason why the whole Christian Church needs a purified catholicism. It should be able to restore to our worship a proper sense of our integrity.

But there is also a seductive aspect to symbols. Symbols have the power to trigger human responses and so they also hook a great range of human sentiment. It is often assumed that the sentiment is true without being trusted. Symbols can be transposed into 'truth' without being tested against the Christian tradition. That is where the radical protest of Protestantism is required. Part of the effectiveness of the Reformation was its questioning of the medieval symbolic world which had often lost touch with Christian truth and human integrity. The symbols were corrupted and no longer ways into salvation. Protestantism could test symbols against theological integrity. The result, one hopes, will not be a renewed iconoclasm but a development of broken symbols.

The broken symbol is a reminder that human beings can only be justified by faith, for we are incomplete, and total certainty is not an option. There is, therefore, a kind of divine restraint which protects us from 'the longing for rest without conflict' (Paul Tillich). This seems to me fundamental to the issue of worship, symbols and human needs. Authentic symbols will protect us from that idealistic longing for certainty without doubt and security without risk. Christian symbols are a reminder of the dividedness both of the world and of the self. The hope in the symbols is that our very brokenness will become the gate of vision and hope. That brokenness is also crucial in preventing us from being manipulated as social puppets by ideologies claiming completeness. Justification by faith preserves our uniqueness and incorporates us into a community in which our mystery is reverenced. *Symbols can protect the boundaries of human life.*

I heard recently from a friend of mine about a baptism he had conducted. He had talked with a girl whose journey had taken her from German Lutheranism through atheism to the Church of England. They discussed her baptism and struggled for a symbol to express something about death and life. They came up with the human heart. It seems to symbolise now so many of the ultimate issues of human life. With coronaries and heart transplants, strokes and heartbreaks it seemed to express something about the ambiguity of death and life. After the preparatory prayers for baptism and the blessing of the water, a drum played out the rhythm of the human heart-beat. Just before the moment of baptism, the drum stopped: the moment of death came. Then as the girl came out of the waters of baptism it began again.

They had looked for a symbol that would unify the tradition of incorporation into the death and resurrection of Jesus with our contemporary experience of living and dying. The ancient symbol of the water and the contemporary symbol of the heart came together in a new logic of relationships. The coherence in that relationship made possible the recognition of a new beginning, a 'change of heart', and related the human and the natural to a world beyond the everyday and observable. It focussed the conviction that at the centre of everything there is a heart, and that heart is human, and that heart is broken, and that heart is God's:

> One of the most important discoveries of the human spirit was naively anticipated when, through certain religious symbols, man guessed that the polarities and antinomies could be articulated as a unity. Since then, the negative and sinister aspects of the cosmos . . . have not only found a justification, but have revealed themselves as an integral part of all reality . . .[11]

If the Christian Church is to rediscover the power of liturgy it must recover the power of symbols and myths. The Church needs to call in humility upon the allied strengths of artists, sculptors, craftspeople, choreographers, musicians and poets to articulate those symbols and myths. But another task needs to be done: we need to work better at the power of 'elaborating' symbols, connecting the disturbing ambiguities of human experience with the ancient symbols. The small beginnings already made lead me to believe that such an endeavour is immensely worthwhile. But I am sceptical whether a church which has become so embedded in the classic Western rationalist tradition can adequately respond. Carl Jung puts his challenge clearly and passionately; I cannot do better than to pass it on again with the conviction that my own pastoral experience underlines every word of it:

> We are surely the rightful heirs of Christian symbolism, but somehow we have squandered this heritage. We have let the house our fathers built fall into decay, and now we try to break into Oriental palaces that our fathers never knew. Anyone who has lost the historical symbols and cannot be satisfied with substitutes is certainly in a very difficult position today: before him yawns the void, and he turns away from it in horror.[12]

1. Mary Douglas, *Natural Symbols* (Penguin 1973), p. 64.
2. Melanie Klein, *Our Adult World and Other Essays* (Heinemann 1963), p. 100.
3. Don Pickard, 'Beneath the Westway', in *Voices from the City* (Thames Television 1982), p. 11.
4. See Sherry B. Ortner, 'On Key Symbols', in *Reader in Comparative Religion*, ed. William Lessa and Evon Vogt (Harper and Row 1979), pp. 92f.
5. Quoted in *The Journal of Pastoral Care*, vol. XXXII, no. 4 (December 1978).
6. Hans Ruedi-Weber, *On a Friday Noon* (SPCK), p. 86.
7. Mircea Eliade, *Patterns in Comparative Religion* (Sheed and Ward 1958), p. 383.
8. Quoted by Owen Chadwick in *The Secularisation of the European Mind in the Nineteenth Century* (Cambridge 1975), p. 35.
9. H. Lambaerts, 'Reciprocal Relationships between Moral Commitment and Faith Profession' in *Towards Moral and Religious Maturity* (Silver Burdett, USA, 1980), p. 255.
10. Chaim Potok, *My Name is Asher Lev* (Heinemann 1972), p. 326.
11. Mircea Eliade, *The History of Religions: Essays in Methodology* (University of Chicago Press 1959), p. 102.
12. C. G. Jung, *Collected Works*, vol. 8 (Routledge 1959), part 1: 'The Archetypes and the Collective Unconscious', p. 15.

6

Grey Grief-Map

Parting is all we know of heaven and all we need to know of hell. (EMILY DICKINSON)

Towards the end of a counselling session, Peter said: 'There are two sides to myself. Right down the middle there is a great gash, a bleeding wound, gory and bloody. What you and I are about here is trying to sew that up, to heal the two sides of myself.' It was one of the most moving symbols that has ever been given to me and struck me as intensely Christian. Peter was struggling, amongst many problems, with issues of loss and separation, remembrance and forgiveness. He began to recognise that there were two sides to himself and that those sides took many forms. I found the image of the bleeding wound powerful because it corresponded closely to the 'bridge', the *corpus collosum*, between the two sides of the brain. It also associated with Jung's 'transcendent principle', which brings about the union of the opposites. But the associations did not stop here. I thought of atonement and of Jesus on the cross, of the bridge, the bleeding wounded Man, uniting us and God in a new kind of anarchic mercy.

The symbol was a vivid reminder that each of us needs to recover our wounded past and find healing in the present and future. We also need to deal with the wounded present in which loss, death and separation are everyday realities. For we spend a great deal of our lives grieving the dream of what never was, what cannot and will never be. We need to be reconciled to what actually is. Worship can be a way and a process of facing the 'great gash' and learning to accept it. When the Church is true to its own vocation, its worship begins to express something of the power of remembrance and forgiveness. Ritual will offer ways of dealing honestly with the past and with loss and separation in the present. If that ritual has integrity it will arise from a community which knows how to deal with failure and death not as someone else's responsibility but as an essential part of our mutuality in penitence and forgiveness. Let me illustrate what I mean by two examples.

An Anglican parish had had a traumatic history. In the course of a few years it had handed over one of its parish churches to another Christian community. Another of its parish churches had been burnt down. The parish priest suffered two major coronaries while the second church was being rebuilt. There were memories of a former curate dying recently from cancer and another being critically ill, and one of the assistant staff was facing a major crisis about the inability of the Church to recognise her great gifts. Part of the dream came to be. The new church was reopened – a creative fusion of the past and the present. But problems remained and the sense of loss persisted. The crisis came to a head on Palm Sunday. A lay person wrote to me: 'Thank God we had the ritual of Holy Week and Easter to contain the pain and breakdown. As we remembered, so restoration and reconciliation began.'

In the second example, a group of women was struggling with the issue of vocation to the priesthood. They talked that struggle through with their diocesan bishop, who agreed that they would present themselves at the next ordination and he would then symbolically turn them away. He believed that that would reflect with integrity how things were. In the event it did not happen because the suffragan bishops would not agree. But I had a question: 'Who was confident that a ritual was available that could have coped with the depth of feeling that would have been discharged had that symbolic act of rejection occurred? What could have contained the anger and rage, tears and horror, resentment and prejudice, hostility and aggression that would have existed in the cathedral at the moment of rejection?' It seemed that both the power of symbol and the weakness of the liturgy to contain such depths of feeling were being ignored.

Those two contrasting examples raise some key questions about grieving and the place of worship in that. Pain and breakdown, loss and death are everyday corporate experiences. They are part of the life of any community and need to be dealt with honestly. We have grown accustomed to thinking about grieving solely in terms of physical death. But dying is about as commonplace as eating and breathing. Dying the small deaths and enduring the lost dreams are bereavements too. In the first example, a community was negotiating its way through a maze of losses and looking for a sign of restoration. The Holy Week liturgy enabled them to do some of that work. It was spacious and strong enough to hold some of the madness.

The second example raises a more acute problem, because it highlights the distance between the theological consciousness of the Church and its conservative practice. There is an almost inevitable hypocrisy in the life of a conservative institution and that creates pastoral crisis. The position of the Anglican Church over the ordination of women is a classic example of this. A conservative institution always has an investment in protecting its own illusory unity against the theological logic of truth. There is a difficulty, therefore, about containing those who grieve what cannot be for them at the moment. Grieving is not just about the past; it is also about the loss of the present. The problem in the Anglican Church is that there are no adequate rituals which can do justice to such a position. It's difficult to see how they could exist. Rituals stem from an integrated theological perspective and have an integrative effect in community. You cannot ritualise a hypocritical position, for ritual is a way of reaffirming the corporate faith of the Christian community. The Anglican ritual of ordination is no longer consistent with what is the declared corporate faith of that community expressed through the General Synod, i.e. that women and men are a gift of grace to each other within one new humanity created in Christ. We need, therefore, a new ritual of ordination which expresses that new order in which opposites are reconciled. We need a healing of 'the great gash', the split that has denied the completeness of Christ's priesthood. I doubt if the Anglican Church can contain for much longer those who grieve what cannot be. But I wonder also how that Church can endure the pain of its own hypocrisy?

Both these examples suggest that we might test the functions of Christian worship against the standpoint of pastoral theology. The Body of Christ is validated by its liturgical effectiveness and becomes what it is when its worship enables the suffering of Jesus to be experienced and the integrity of Jesus to be recognised. If we take the image of the Body of Christ seriously, we shall believe in Worship as an environment to live in, an environment in which the integrity of Jesus is actually known. In that sense the Church's present practice of ordination in the Anglican and Roman Catholic Churches is a departure from catholic truth and as such is a dishonest business. As a ritual, it cannot care for people because it does not reconcile the opposites. It excludes those who could make it whole:

> The one feature of the Church which really can be universal and which can represent its mission in all circumstances, is that the Church is a praying presence of the continuing humanity of the Son of God in the world. It is the presence in the world of a group of people who, through persistent and perhaps secret acts of worship, are seeking to bring their values into line with the nature of God, and who therefore are sharing something of God's compassion, anger, and hope for the created order of which they are a part.   (J. D. Davies)[1]

I want to look now at the funeral as a focus for grief. This subject has been dealt with in *Letting Go* by Ian Ainsworth-Smith and Peter Speck, and I agree substantially with their conclusions and do not intend to repeat them here.[2] I do want, however, to make a series of further points about the ways in which the funeral liturgy cares for people and how some contemporary liturgies fail to achieve that.

Death can often be surrounded by guilt. This is especially true when death has happened suddenly or when it happens through suicide. But it is not only traumatic endings that leave untidy ends. The social fragmentation of Western society and the growth of the global village have led to families living many miles, if not continents, apart from each other. Sons and daughters may only be able to return for the funeral itself. There are few families where there is not unfinished business. There may not have been opportunities for reconciliations, for forgiveness, for mutual honesty and new acceptance. I have taken more than one funeral where I have stood between two warring groups at a graveside. A death has a way of bringing the latent hostility in many families out into the open. A funeral conducted in the Christian tradition is like all other liturgy. It is a sign that all things and all people have been reconciled in Christ. It is a means of helping people deal with their guilt and their unfinished business.

I think it is a matter of concern, therefore, that the Anglican Alternative Service Book is extremely reticent on the issue of guilt and forgiveness. No opportunity is given in the funeral rite for public confession of sin and an act of absolution. It deprives people of dealing with matters which are central to their health. There is a prayer which says; 'Lead us to repent of our sins, the evil we have done and the good we have not done',[3] but there is no act of confession and absolution. It is, in one sense, a non-involving liturgy. The overall impression is of prayer being said over the congregation rather than a liturgical act in which the congregation is actively involved. I recognise on the one hand how difficult it is for many mourners to participate when their grief is so profound. But on the other hand liturgies can often be examples of pastoral deprivation and I believe that the Anglican funeral liturgy is just such an example. It has to be admitted that the 1662 liturgy was no better. Much of the debate about new liturgy has been about the directness of our speech to God. I wish that more of that debate had been about our honesty before God.

This issue is important in another respect. Funerals are often community events. The Church needs to be circumspect about colluding with the privatisation of grief in the Western world. A funeral is a public act of Christian worship and in many circumstances it will be an opportunity for members of the community to do their own preparation for death and their unfinished business. I remember one community in which I was a curate. Two very tragic deaths had occurred in one family. The first son had died in a road accident. The parents could not grieve the death and the whole community colluded with their daily visits to the grave and its adornment with the most expensive flowers. When the second son died of leukaemia two years later, there was an opportunity for not only the parents but the whole community to confront the reality of death and to grieve appropriately. Liturgy can be an opportunity to bring issues out into the open with pastoral sensitivity, but it has to be an honest statement of how things actually are. Anything which hides the reality of death may be pastoral deprivation for a whole community.

The funeral liturgy in the Anglican Church and in some other traditions has the weakness of a lot of contemporary liturgy. Instead of particular structures and words which have to be used in all pastoral circumstances, we need a resource book which can be used flexibly. If the leading of worship could be appropriately restored to the heart of priesthood, those who lead it would be freed to work out with those to whom they minister the content of the funeral liturgy. Many people do make requests for specific readings or solos, for example, but it seems to me odd that only certain psalms are recommended. They are useful starting points, but there are others which are penetrating confessions of honesty and hope, and which might be more appropriate in particular pastoral circumstances. Following the logic of my last chapter there also needs to be some hard work done on the place of symbols in the funeral liturgy. Even simple acts, like the removal of the pall and the asperging of the coffin, heighten the symbolism. One of the most powerful funerals I ever officiated at was for a gypsy; many small symbolic acts and the ritual wailing freed people to grieve the end of a whole network of relationships. Symbols, actions and movements conveyed the power of a *rite de passage*, of a movement from one state of being to another, not only for the dead person but for the community of which they had been a part. Part of the community had died as well.

There are occasions when grieving has to be managed on a much wider scale: a nation or a group of nations has to make sense of its complicity in the systemic violence of the world where it is difficult to distinguish between the oppressor and the victim. Remembrance Sunday is a well established attempt to make some sense of war and peace. In these

circumstances there is a risk that we shall idealise the victims
to avoid our own complicity in oppression:

> I 'atone' for my primal sin of oppression by according a
> superior instead of an inferior place to my victims, placing
> a moral scourge in their hands to beat me as once I beat
> them; and this is a travesty of the process of human
> reconciliation and restoration; my imagination is still
> trapped in the illusion that the basic and ultimate form
> of human relation is that between the powerful and the
> powerless.   (Rowan Williams)[4]

The remembrance of things past focusses corporate pastoral
needs. It also raises the difficult area of forgetting and
forgiving. Any society needs ways of dealing with that remembrance, and our society has enlisted the Church's aid in
rituals of remembrance. Those rituals are not without ambiguity, and they may not be the most appropriate way of
enabling the post-Hiroshima generations to deal with their
own remembrance of violence and their vision of peace. The
Church's ritual needs to answer the accusation of the
professor's son in Morris West's *The Clowns of God*: 'We were
angry with you and your generation because you had a past
to look back on while we had only a question mark before
us.'[5]

The memorial service after the Falklands war in 1982
focussed on some of the inherent problems in dealing with
human questions about war and peace and the fears endemic
in both. The difficulties that are always there in Remembrance Sundays were reflected in the arguments. We need
help in dealing with the disintegration of the past and the
creation of the future. But ritual has some contradictions built
into it, for it functions in more than one way. In many
societies it is used as a sanctification of the socio-ethical code.
It ensures society's cohesion and provides a way for individuals to sacrifice their self-interest to the wider interests of the
community. That strengthens the survival of the group. The
ethical and liturgical imperatives may even lead individuals
to die for the community. It does seem that Remembrance
Sunday has had much of this character about it. Certainly
some of the demands of the Conservative government at the
time of the Falklands service fell into this category.

But there is another form of ritual. That is about perceiving a transcendent purpose enabling individuals to share in a community influenced by the imperatives of peace. If we take the norm of Christian worship already defined in this chapter – that is, worship enables the suffering of Jesus to be experienced and his integrity to be recognised – then we will have to ask some different questions about Remembrance Sunday. This raises a distinction between public and corporate worship. The distinction seemed to be delineated sharply in the debate surrounding the liturgy in St Paul's Cathedral after the Falklands war. Many sections of society, including the government, recognised a need to deal with the aftermath of the war and demanded a liturgy largely couched in terms of celebration and thanksgiving. The Anglican Church might have colluded with that had it not been for the influence of Cardinal Basil Hume and Dr Kenneth Greet, who insisted that the liturgy must spell out something of the reconciliation and peace achieved by Jesus and the demands that arise from that for the Church to be a peace-making community. It seems to me that this ambiguity in ritual runs through many local debates about worship, especially in those areas where there is a strong adherence to traditional values. Many parishioners look to their local parish Church for the sanctification of their particular social-ethical code.

The Church, therefore, has a difficult problem. It needs to be able to respond to the corporate dilemmas of loss and grief and the pastoral needs that arise from those. It is an integral part of the Christian mission to interpret the signs of the times and to minister in judgement and hope both to the victim and the oppressor, and that must find a place in worship. Part of the ambiguity about the service after the Falklands war was the degree to which Britain had in fact committed the primal act of oppression by seizing the Falklands in the first place. There was much more ambiguity between victim and oppressor than was allowed for.

This suggests that the time has also come for a radical overhaul of Remembrance Day services. The answer is not to do away with them, as has happened in so many local churches. The question we need to ask is: how can we deal with an annual act of remembrance without it being simply a sanctification of one particular social code? It is interesting that there have been many local experiments which have tried to take account of changing perceptions whilst the national service remains almost totally fossilised. The Church of England needs to ask some very radical questions about its collusion with this service. The whole Church might ask how the Feast of the Transfiguration, August 6th, which is also the anniversary of the bombing of Hiroshima, could be restored to a more prominent place in the Church's liturgical life. That feast poses precisely the question that is before the whole of humanity: will it be adoration or annihilation? The Church is there to deal with the remembrance of things past so that we might be creators of a new future: in that sense Christian liturgy has a precise parallel in pastoral counselling:

> People often say: 'You should forget all about your unhappy experiences, just put them out of your mind and you will be all right'. This may work in the short term, but as a long-term measure it is very bad advice, even if it were actually possible to make a conscious decision to forget. The things we want to forget have a nasty habit of forcing their way back into consciousness in one form or another, sometimes directly when we least expect them and are off our guard and sometimes, in dreams, faulty action, irrational fears or phantasies or in bodily symptoms.
> (I. Bloomfield)[6]

The body politic is not immune from the same problem.

A distinction between corporate and public worship may help us discern some of the difficulties in one of the major books that has been written on human need and religious ritual, *The Dynamics of Religion* by Bruce Reed. In that book Reed performs the important task of trying to analyse what actually happens in worship. He discusses, through the oscillation theory, the two different ways that people have of experiencing the world: the first is a way of dealing with present and future realities in the public world; the second is a state of dependence in which a person looks beyond for a person or object to provide confirmation, protection and sustenance.[7] The purpose of Christian ritual becomes a way of handling the anxieties experienced in the public world so that individuals and groups can carry on with those tasks on which the survival of society depends. It seems to me that

that definition of worship is almost totally dependent upon an understanding of ritual as the sanctification of particular socio-ethical codes. He is dealing, therefore, not with corporate worship, which explicates the primary task of the Christian Church, but with worship understood as public ritual. John Montague in a review of the book concludes: 'I find it doubly difficult to accept when a whole apparatus of psycho-analytical and organisational tools ends up by fashioning a structure which looks suspiciously like the status quo of forty years ago in liturgy and pastoralia alike.'[8]

Christian liturgy is committed to those who suffer for the cause of human liberation and justice in the name of the Victim, Jesus Christ. It will always raise critical questions about those who use it for 'extra dependence' or for the sanctification of a particular set of public values. Christian worship is a sign on the way to establish the Kingdom of Peace.

I want to turn now to look at one particular group whom we discover on our grey grief-map: old people. There is a remarkable contrast between the story of Pentecost, where old people will 'dream dreams', and the place of old people in our own society where they are often pushed to the margins of society. In a world where increasingly large numbers of people live longer, both Church and society will be faced with choices about the place of old people in the community. What is already clear is that those elderly people pose fundamental questions about worth and dignity. I have heard it said more than once by professional clerics: 'Oh don't bother preparing an address; there will only be six old ladies and a cat.' That does not seem to be about old people being restored to a place 'to dream dreams'. Retirement seems to be a life crisis that people find particularly difficult to navigate. That is inevitable, I suppose, in a society addicted to a work ethic which evaluates people by what they produce and the resources they earn. But it is not New Testament faith: in that perspective, those who are stripped of their worth are restored to the centre of the human stage by the Spirit of Jesus:

No longer will the Spirit be restricted to 'significant' people for special tasks and occasions, as in the Old Testament dispensation. The Spirit is now being shared by the whole community, including the young, the old and the slaves – three groups who get shoved into the margins of society. (J. D. Davies)[9]

The case-study at the beginning of chapter 1 raises most of the questions about how liturgy can care for elderly people. The basic theological question will be one about their value and from where they derive it. The liturgy can be a vehicle of God's grace if it takes account of their pastoral needs. Those who lead worship will need sensitivity to the memories of old people. New rites should not be imposed simply because they are now the common use of the Church. Flexibility will be needed as a minister grows to know a group better. Elderly people can reflect if they are taken at their own pace; it should not be assumed in a geriatric ward that people are incapable of responding simply because they are semi-conscious or senile. There is more to any human being than conscious or rational speech. To sit silently holding the hand of an old person in the presence of God is to worship. Ritual acts like anointing with oil are able to reach deeper than rational speech. The Lord's Prayer said slowly and lovingly may touch depths of personality hardly recognised by anyone else. If we are serious in believing that people can respond to God up to and through death, our liturgy in an old people's home or a geriatric ward will be radically affected. It can open *inner* eyes and ears to a vision of the Kingdom.

This leads me to suggest that there are in fact four theological variables which enable us to diagnose what is an authentic event of Christian worship in any circumstance:

1. By marking out the boundary of the holy, worship is a statement of where God is active in mission. The Church is called to identify with God wherever he is bringing his love and hope to birth in the world. We are challenged about our ultimate loyalties through that.

2. By mediating the grace of God, worship helps us appre-

hend grace in a concrete and specific way. We can relate honestly to God and trust him enough to share some of our loss of dignity, or frustration and anger, or joy and peace. If we cannot express all we are, we may be blocked from receiving God's grace.

3. By promoting faith, worship is an opportunity for us to make new commitments. One of the strengths of new liturgy is that it helps us see more clearly what is at stake and to make honest choices based on that. Membership of Christian congregations does not necessarily signify faith, but good liturgy will help people sort out their choices and priorities and so act more honestly.

4. By offering a structure which enables us to make our response to God, whatever our human condition, worship deepens corporate communion and human vocation. It helps us recognise, in the words of St Augustine: 'That is you being placed on the altar, along with your gifts.' It enhances our sense of vocation, including the vocation to die.

We all have a grey grief-map; a means of discerning sense in the midst of meaninglessness and chaos. I have talked about grieving what has not been and what cannot be. I want to end by reflecting about grieving what will never be. It may seem odd to put grief and the future into a single perspective. But it is a strange strand of much human experience that certain things will never be. They need to be grieved as well. I believe that Christian worship enables us to do that because it is eschatological: it recognises that what has taken place in Jesus is in some way the story of the future. That is a perspective in which I can begin to embrace the potentiality that will not be realised until the end time when all things will be restored to their full stature. In worship we can examine the distorted maps of our own cosmos and make honest choices about our future. Those honest choices are made in the recognition that through worship my worth is restored to me by God. That begins to free me to let go of everything, including the dreams of the future, that can never be. There are many people who need that liberation because they are living with dreams of the future that can never be realised. They vary

from the spiritually barren curate who harbours dreams of
being a bishop to the gay woman who longs to have children.
Christian worship at its best frees us from those illusions and
gives us space to grieve what will never be. In that way the
grey grief-map leads us to the land of peace:

> . . . it is always possible for everyone to go further-deeper.
> And to go deeper into the reality of what is inevitably
> leads away from the self, away from the power-hungry ego,
> towards a more comprehensive map of the cosmos, one
> that ultimately makes an anthropocentric world view
> impossible.   (J. Fortunato).[10]

1. John D. Davies, *The Faith Abroad* (Basil Blackwell 1983), p. 150.
2. Ian Ainsworth-Smith and Peter Speck, *Letting Go* (SPCK), p. 61f. See
   especially chapter 5: 'Rites and Customs', dealing specifically with: (i)
   the funeral as a *rite de passage*; (ii) care of the dying; (iii) the funeral
   service; (iv) pre-funeral visiting; (v) post-funeral care; (vi) children
   and funerals.
3. Alternative Service Book (Hodder and Stoughton 1980), 'The Funeral
   Service', p. 314.
4. Rowan Williams, *Resurrection* (Darton Longman & Todd 1982), p. 17.
5. Morris West, *The Clowns of God* (Hodder & Stoughton 1981), pp. 155–6.
6. Irene Bloomfield, in the *APCC Journal*, no. 3 (Spring 1983), pp. 18–19.
7. See Bruce Reed, *The Dynamics of Religion* (Darton, Longman & Todd
   1978).
8. John Montague, in *Crucible* (The Journal of the General Synod Board
   for Social Responsibility), April-June 1979, p. 94.
9. John D. Davies, *The Faith Abroad* (Basil Blackwell 1983), p. 24.
10. John Fortunato, *Embracing the Exile* (Seabury Press 1982), p. 100.

Reclothing the Dream

did the woman say,
when she hailed him for the last time in
the dark rain on a hilltop,
After the pain and the bleeding and the dying,
'this is my body; this is my blood'?

well that she said it to him then,
for dry old men,
brocaded robes belying barrenness,
ordain that she not say it for him now.
(FRANCIS FRANK: 17th-century Roman Catholic
priest)

The liturgical and sexual revolutions are out of step with each other. As the Anglican Church settled down to travel to 2000 AD, with the Alternative Service Book, women were breaking through into a new vision of the Body of Christ. There is a stream of Christian spirituality which has taken human sexuality seriously as a way of expressing our relationship to God. But that spirituality has hardly affected Christian liturgy at all. It highlights both the conservative nature of liturgy and how liturgy reflects the Church. Some recent writing on the renewal of worship manages to sidestep the issue, but it cannot be avoided from a pastoral perspective.[1] The issue cannot be ignored, because of the part that sexuality plays in the whole formation of human personality. In addition, Christian orthodoxy claims that a wholly new state of affairs in the relationships between women and men has been brought about by Jesus. If worship really does care for people, there are unavoidable questions about the forms and language in which that worship is expressed.

I would like to begin with sexist language in Liturgy. I do not believe it is the fundamental issue but it is the symptom that most clearly indicates that there is a problem. I felt it would be intolerable if this was yet another book written by a man about women so I invited a number of women to write to me about the question. Here is a selection of comments from what they wrote:

> In Christ Jesus is found the supreme symbol, the Interpreter of Incarnation. God's activity in his Person-hood, life, death and resurrection gives ultimate terms of reference to the human journey. In Jesus we find the image of humanity and God in such a way that joint being and common language is comprehended.   (Methodist minister/ priest)

> It is not language, though that is vicious enough, and it's not only the misuse of symbols, like that cardboard character, the BVM, and not only sexist Bible stories, but the fact that the patriarchal society, which prevents the full humanity of most women, is at its most acute in this bloody institution that pretends to have the Gospel of liberation into wholeness and fullness of life. Well it has but it seems to be dedicated to keeping women down.   (Anglican lay reader)

> The other side of the question is, of course, language about God and the need for words and images to convey the 'feminine' face of God.   (member of the World Council of Churches)

> Language determines our thoughts as well as reflecting it, so if we don't make a conscious effort to correct sexual stereotypes and sexist language in the liturgy (as elsewhere) our attitudes won't change . . . I don't think concern about language is trivial. It signifies and symbolises a great deal, as debate about language in liturgy shows.   (Roman Cath-olic nun)

> Liturgy has been controlled and formed by male priests on

the whole and language can be a powerful instrument of exclusion or inclusion . . . At the core of the whole problem is the fact that liturgy has been used by a caste or an elite and by the conquering nations so that people have been pushed out of their true place within the worshipping community. (Anglican deaconess)

Occasionally there has been an opportunity to highlight and draw attention to the problem. For example, when drafting during the Revision of the Service for the Sick, I used 'her' rather than 'him' as the narrative pronoun in the Service of Laying on of Hands and Anointing. The reaction, which I both expected and accepted, was an appeal to the 'rules' and conventions of English grammar, by which the masculine form is always deemed the normative. But it made the point. (member of the Anglican Liturgical Commission)

It is no use pretending that there are simple answers to this dilemma. There are not. If we are to discover more holistic ways of imagining both God and ourselves, it will not be a simple process of recovering a biblical language or creating a new language. It will be part of a much wider process in which women and men discover how to imagine being in God together. Both women and men need space to discover who they are so that they can release each other from feminine and masculine stereotypes. That process will cause much pain, but it may help us find the 'Motherly Father' (Jurgen Moltmann) who is at the heart of the cross of Jesus. We need to help each other find that space to be ourselves if we are to be more whole. But in the end we cannot avoid the issue of language.

There is a double difficulty here. How do we speak about ourselves in liturgy? How do we address God? The first problem can be remedied to some extent. I never hesitate to substitute the word 'people' when 'men' is used or 'humanity' for 'mankind'. In many small ways quite radical changes could be effected immediately. Those who have the responsibility for leading intercessions or preaching sermons can be alert to their own use of sexist language. The appeals to the normative usage of male language are meaningless because that usage is itself the product of a patriarchal culture. The following examples illustrate possible alternatives:

> his perfect sacrifice made once for the sins of all men (people). (Anglican Holy Communion Rite A: 3rd Eucharist Prayer)

> Do you believe and trust in his Son Jesus Christ who redeemed mankind (everyone). (Anglican Baptism)

> We praise and thank you, Lord of heaven and earth; you are the hope and joy of men (and women) in every age. (Roman Catholic Morning and Evening Prayer)

> A deacon assists the priest under whom he (or she/or 'she or he') serves. (Anglican Ordination of Deacons)

There are numerous examples that could be cited. There are very few places where the liturgical text would be violated by a simple amendment of language. Sara Maitland in a study of the relationship of spirituality and language focusses how this exploration could lead women and men into a fresh understanding of themselves and God:

> There is a deep way in which it could be natural for men to seek God through female images and women to seek God through male language, because – if we abandoned the projection and denial game – that could become a natural expression of Otherness. This cannot happen while either side of the balanced difference is perceived at any level as being 'better than', 'superior to' or 'more holy than' the other.[2]

If worship is to care for everyone it needs to find a language which does not 'reveal that they have never included us' (Helen Schmidt).

The metaphors of masculinity which dominate liturgical texts need to be progressively reduced because they are also unfair to men. It will be a difficult struggle because language and society are intimately bound together, but when a more inclusive language is used in society, liturgy will be affected by that. There is another significant change, however, already taking place, which will also be decisive. Liturgical language is the product of our experience of the living God rather than the official God of state religion. As more and more experiments take place in which women and men explore their spirituality, so new languages about God and ourselves will emerge. A useful criterion by which those languages may be judged is suggested by Keith Watkins in his book on sexist language in worship:

> Thus the first interim principle that can guide our striving for truth and justice in Christian worship is this: during the transitional period our goal should be the development of liturgical language that is fair to women as well as to men and that is faithful to our experience of God.[3]

There is a more profound difficulty when we turn to language about God, which is a difficult enough subject in itself. Hermeneutical studies of liturgical language reveal that it arose in a socio-political context which was male-dominated. Biblical language and translations and Western liturgical rites are the products of social systems in which men held the power. It is not surprising, therefore, that language about God reflects that. Some Christian spirituality has thrown up a much greater richness of imagery:

> As truly as God is our father, so just as truly is he our mother.
> It is I, the strength and goodness of fatherhood.
> It is I, the wisdom of motherhood.
> It is I, the light and grace of holy love.
> It is I, the Trinity, it is I, the unity.
>
> (Julian of Norwich)

But Christian liturgy does not yet reflect that richness.

Perhaps the clue to a new point of departure lies in that quotation from Julian of Norwich. If we could recover a much fuller Trinitarian language we might have that flexibility we need. All language about ourselves in relationship to God has both the dimension of uniqueness and the dimension of communion (see also chapters 1 and 2). In the new struggle between women and men and God it is precisely that dialectic between uniqueness and communion which we need to hold onto. It is a dialectic which exists in the Christian view of God's nature: ' . . . I have learnt that the idea of the Trinity is based on something that can be experienced and must, therefore, have a meaning'   (C. G. Jung).[4]

Trinitarian language offers us the kind of flexibility that we are seeking, because through it we can explore a whole number of symbols of God. We are further aided in that by the reminder that in ancient Hebrew 'spirit' was always a feminine noun. The exploration of a wide range of metaphors and symbols for God may release us from the patriarchal 'Father' as an almost exclusive way of addressing God. Here is one example of the potentiality within Trinitarian language: 'Life-Giver, Pain-Bearer, Love-maker'.[5] Another possibility might be: God, Lover, Pioneer, Giver of Courage. It would be a good test for many congregations to draw out a storehouse of imagery from a Trinitarian understanding of God which could be used with integrity by women and men alike. Words are a source of power. Language determines at very deep levels what we believe and how we create. That exploration might also lead many Christians back into a much fuller understanding of trinitarian faith.

One further point needs to be made about God language from a pastoral angle. Nothing will be solved by simply substituting Mother for Father. Anybody who is in the business of pastoral counselling knows that both symbols are highly charged and extremely ambiguous. Mother is even more likely to focus destructive feelings because our experience of Mother is more basic than the experience of Father. Most people carry at least four parents inside themselves; a bad and a good Mother and a bad and good Father. That highlights in a very simple way how liturgical language might be both disturbing and liberating.

Beneath the issue of language there is a more fundamental problem which is likely to prove much more threatening to the Church, but women and men will only be free if it is resolved. It is the issue of the images of leadership within the Church and its liturgies. The issue is not simply about correcting human and God language. It is also about creating changes in the way in which God is imaged within the liturgy. Radical changes are required in the power structures and leadership of the Church if it is to be faithful to the biblical

vision of the co-equality in priesthood of women and men
before God (Genesis 1:27; Galatians 3:27–8). The Church
talks about itself as a servant Church, but it is very difficult
to detect the operational effectiveness of that theological
conviction. If we are to take the image of the Body of Christ
seriously, we have to examine the fact that in most churches
men still hold the leadership. That usually means they also
hold the power. This is focussed sharply in the leadership of
the liturgy. For that reason alone some men will need to offer
themselves as the servants of women in the struggle to change
the icon of leadership within the Church. It is bound to be a
threatening process and will be met with much resistance:
'For every woman who takes a step towards her own liberation, there is a man who finds the way to freedom has been
made a little easier' (Nancy Smith).[6]

In the transitional period we will need pastoral and
educational strategies if we are to develop a more inclusive
language. There is bound to be resistance to changes in
language because people will feel that their understanding of
God is under threat (see also chapters 1 and 2). Ministers
already have a limited range of freedom in the use of liturgical
texts. They could be more sensitive about their use of
language in sermons, notices and extempore prayers. Many
attempts could be made to give women and men greater
equality in both traditional and experimental liturgies. More
teaching could be given about the Christian perspective on
the roles of women and men so that dialogues are promoted
and new conversations begun. In private prayer, individuals
could be encouraged to personalise their words for God. As
we have nicknames for each other, why could we not develop
our own personal names for God? We could support and
encourage each other in that mutual freedom and justice that
women and men both need in order to be ministers of the
Gospel. There are numerous pastoral and educational strategies available for us to develop a much more inclusive
language and community.

It would, however, be dishonest in a book reflecting on the
relationship of liturgy and pastoral care, not to raise one
question. There is a continuity between feminine and masculine archetypes but there are also clear differences. Those
differences stem from psychological as well as ethological

roots. Men and women will need to go on embodying those archetypes in both Church and society if human health is to be promoted. Both female and male patterns are central to individual health. They are also necessary for the growth of human institutions. Women are not likely to promote human health according to the life of Christ, by simply adopting the characteristics of male dominated clericalism. Women will need to bring that combination of generous altruism, creative nurturing and intimate strength, which are all characteristics of the feminine archetype, if leadership in the Church is to be consistent with human integrity. We must expect that women will radically change our whole symbolic grasp of leadership. We need to heed this warning from Anthony Stevens:

> Although recent moves in the matrist direction have corrected this repressive tendency to a large extent, it is, nevertheless, an interesting paradox that the women's movement is unwittingly compounding the patrist felony by extolling the virtues of work and ambition while disparaging those of love, care-giving and motherhood: in other words, they are worshipping masculine attributes and condemning feminine ones.[7]

There is a further symbol, much overused in church circles, which has this same power to include or exclude. It is the ambiguous symbol of the family (see also chapter 4). Churches have family services, family communions, family euchar-ists, family days. Few, I think, realise how oppressive that is to many people. I know what the defence will be. We are talking about the family of God and that is an all embracing, inclusive human community. But the evidence counts against the defence. If we test the reality again by its operational effectiveness, it seems that the Western Church is being seduced into life patterns that are privatised and exclusive. The family has become a key symbol embodying the values and morality of a society; in fact some sociologists claim that it now has a religious connotation because it has replaced God as the primary source of values. But the family can also be the source of violence and breakdown, of the profoundest human pain. The family, too, has two sides to it.

The Church, on the whole, is not very good at recognising, let alone reconciling, the polarities within the family. One consequence is that the image of the family, used in liturgy, can become a kind of suffocating maternalism. It excludes some people and makes them feel unacceptable. It is a world away from the Jesus who sat down with a rag-bag of humanity to share stories and food. Many churches remind me of the landscape drawn by the poet Stevie Smith: a land in which net curtains and laurel hedges protect people from reality, and for good measure a ginger tom-cat sometimes guards the territorial imperative. Some sides-people and church-wardens remind me of ginger toms and tortoiseshell cats! The family has become a refuge in a world which is too demanding and the Church colludes with this. Pieces of land and piles of brick become the way to tell the Christian story, and the privacy of it all violates human life. Try for one moment to empathise with a widower or a single person, a single parent or a gay person and to imagine what this obsession with the family means for them. We have forgotten what Jesus highlighted: the family needs to be redeemed as well (Matthew 12:46–50). Because liturgy sometimes has this exclusive character, many people, who want to embrace Christian faith, sing their songs of silent pain in exile. I know because I know lots of them. Society has a way of splitting off those parts it cannot cope with. There are many ghettoes, places which hold the pain of those with whom we cannot cope. From San Francisco to Brixton, from mental hospital to homeless shelter, the ministry of hospitality needs to be extended to the exiles.

We look instead for a liturgy that will reflect the movement of God in Jesus: a movement that began on the margins of society and took humanity into the very heart of God. In that single movement the worth and value of those who feel exiled was changed for ever. It broke open all the predictable norms and patterns and established a 'new creation', a totally new kind of human community, for which the symbol of 'family' is hopelessly inadequate. In Jesus, life which was despised and potential which was unused was brought into effective action. Its value was restored at the heart of human life and all the categories and definitions with which we choose to label people were called into question. Jesus freed people to take their humanity into God. *Could there be a better definition of Christian liturgy? The freedom to take our humanity into God.* It is in the heart of Christian orthodoxy that the humanity of Jesus has made a final difference. It has made an irreversible difference to God. Liturgy which expresses this Easter mystery will play a part in the reversal of the world's values. It will be about the solidarity of friendship rather than the exclusivity of the Western family. I hope that many Christian congregations will question radically the ways in which they describe their worship and activities.

In contrast to this, we need to look at how the Church does prepare people for the ambiguity of family life. The marriage service provides a useful focus. Like all *rites de passage*, it clarifies the values and concepts that the Christian Church holds about marriage. The ritual is, therefore, a preparation for a new status in life and, like all *rites de passage*, it brings about the new status through three stages: separation, transition, incorporation. Those three stages are useful ways of looking at how the marriage liturgy cares for women and men.

The marriage liturgy is a ritualised celebration of sexual union, although one might not always think so when listening to many church debates about marriage. The threatening, mysterious power of human sexuality is avoided with many ambivalent words. The Church still distrusts human sexuality and will go to endless lengths to 'protect the faithful' from what they recognise to be one of the most powerful forces in their life. In contrast, the marriage liturgy claims that sexual union is a joyous sign of God's continuing love and a sign of creation. The new Anglican marriage liturgy has clarified the celebration of sexual union: 'It is God's purpose that, as husband and wife give themselves to each other in love throughout their lives, they shall be united in that love as Christ is united with his Church.'[8] What the new liturgy has sacrificed is an honest recognition of the ambiguity of human sexuality. Although the 1662 Anglican liturgy was at fault in many ways, it did show a more realistic grasp of the destructive, as well as creative, power of sexuality: ' . . . to satisfy men's carnal lusts and appetites, like brute beasts that have no understanding'.[9] The new Anglican liturgies have an aura of middle-class respectability about them. But you do not have to wander far in any city to recognise that the 1662 liturgy also had part of the truth. Can liturgy care for people if it does not recognise honestly the ambiguous nature of human sexuality?

The phase of separation begins in the preparation for the ritual. This can bring out the fact that the woman and man are separating from families and their relationship will depend on the success of this separation. When a woman and a man get into bed with each other, all too often four others leap in as well: the respective mothers and fathers they carry inside themselves. The new liturgy makes this provision: 'The priest may receive the bride from the hands of her father.' There is more reticence here than in the old liturgy and all notions of 'handing over the goods' need to be avoided. But the necessity for both woman and man to separate from their parents must be recognised. Mothers can be just as tenacious at hanging on to sons as fathers to daughters! We may not always recognise the pastoral significance of the ritual separation. At a recent marriage at which I officiated, I was horrified to see the bride rejoining her father after the marriage had taken place. I blushed at how abysmally my preparation had failed!

The phase of transition is effected by a series of symbolic acts which reflect the Church's convictions about love. The vows spell out what are the requirements for any deep, lasting friendship, of which heterosexual marriage is one form. It is quite common in some Christian traditions for couples to ask if they can compose their own marriage liturgy. Most good liturgy is a delicate balance of structure and flexibility. Ministers may need to remember that Christian liturgy is an expression of the whole church and that the ritual is supremely an act of worship. But more importantly the exchange of vows is a clear statement about the nature of love. The vows are indicators of what the Christian community believes to be the conditions for a wholly human friendship, and spell out the character of the permanence of love and the mutuality of risk in a new relationship. That same quality is captured in some of the new covenants of friendship, which some gay people use to celebrate their commitment to each other:

'I embrace you, choosing and being chosen to share with you my being and becoming . . . I promise to be for you and for your well-being for ever, to honour you as a dwelling place of God, and to be loyal to you and full of faith in you, our life day long.'[10]

The whole marriage ritual is an act of incorporation into the wider community. Christian liturgy is a community event, however much ministers may be pressured into turning it into a private occasion. It is an act of proclamation about God's grace, which operates in the face of failure and breakdown, and is an opportunity for all members of the community to renew their bonds of friendship. Like funeral rites, it enables the wider community to deal with the business of living.

Here it is necessary to deal, at least briefly, with the question of the marriage of divorced people. Much store is placed today on premarital counselling and marriage preparation as a prevention of marriage breakdown. In fact a good deal of it may reveal our mistrust of the liturgy to do its own work. But the focus is useful in another way. I would want to argue that in most marriage breakdowns the sin was in the genesis and not in the failure. I realise that may be an unusual theological position, but my own marriage breakdown and my counselling of others leads me to believe that it is true. The sin is in the illusions, the lack of self-awareness and the failure in honesty which lead people into marriage. Talking through the liturgy as a preparation may expose some of the illusions and lack of self-awareness, but the failures will still happen.

Any procedures that the Church adopts for the marriage of divorced people must therefore always operate in the highest pastoral interests of the couple concerned. If I am right in believing that the sin lies in the genesis rather than in the failure of a marriage, there will be a need for rigorous care at the beginning of a new one. But I believe it to be pastorally damaging to deny people the possibility of new grace in the face of their failure. The Free Churches, on the whole, have been prepared to take more risks, but the ambiguity about the sacramental nature of vows in the Anglican and Roman Catholic Churches adds to the confusion. The Anglican Church has tried unsuccessfully to resolve this problem. What is clear is that ritual can play a primary part in the re-creation of life after failure and breakdown. The Church is not often clear that the proclamation of the good news of grace is more important than its own fastidious conscience. New marriage after divorce is a prime example of liturgy and pastoral care being allies together in building the foundations of new life.

If Christian worship is to encourage whole people to express the whole gospel in the whole world by enabling us to find our own worth in God, it has to be embodied worship. It means literally taking our bodies seriously. The presence of God needs to be en-fleshed in us. Our flesh is a reminder too that there is no part of our humanity, including our sexuality, which is not a vehicle for the adoration of God. Human bodies tell many stories about human health. If worship is to care for us it must allow space for that body language too.

It can begin in very simple ways. I am struck by the frequent failure of clergy to use their bodies in worship. The different stages of the great eucharistic prayer can be emphasised by different body movements. Those movements need to correspond with the actual meaning of the prayer. Like all choreography, word and movement need to be integrated. The whole body can be bent into a position of deep submission at the Sanctus. The arms can be raised to full height at the declaration of the mystery of faith: 'Christ has died. Christ is risen. Christ will come again.' Through the action, the Word is embodied: it would be deeply moving if a congregation began to be caught up into such a choreography.

The body can be used to highlight different forms of prayer. Posture and stance can express a whole variety of attitudes towards God from profound penitence to exaltant adoration. They begin to express the unity of the self before God:

> The highest function of the body in prayer is to provide a language . . . using one's body in every possible way to express the deep things of life is a great art indeed. This is true in the relationship between people; it is no less true in that between man and God.   (H. Caffarel)[11]

The use of the body can inspire a fresh attitude to God because it can make the whole self more alert and attentive to the divine presence. In order to do that, we may well need to pay more attention to our bodies through relaxation and exercise so that the whole self can find its true home in God. The liturgy is itself a movement and a dance, and frequently dance and movement can enhance that. Indeed liturgical dance and movement has done much to re-establish embodied worship. That dance needs first of all to enhance the structure of the liturgy and not blur its clear lines. It must also enable the congregation to participate more fully in the *mysterium tremendum*. Like choral performances, liturgical dance can simply be a piece of ego-tripping for those who like that sort of thing. But music and movement are the servants of the people of God which, through discipline and skill, enable people to be touched by God. Much greater thought could be given to miming, dramatising and dancing the gospel stories. Liturgical dance can heighten the movement of the gospel reading or offertory procession, and can deepen silence into stillness, and stillness into contemplation. Those who use these skills are ministering to others in their wholeness. We are raised beyond ourselves into the presence of the Kingdom, which is the universe recreated according to the purposes of God: 'Prayer is the direction and renewal of the whole person . . . and this involves our bodies. Our bodies are channels to receive and give out this divine energy.' (M. Craighead)[12]

Within the stream of Christian spirituality, there is a continuous flow between sensuality and prayer. In many of the greatest writers, like Julian of Norwich, Thomas Merton and St Theresa of Lisieux, there is a refreshing recognition that human sexuality is one means of adoring God. In the solitude and silence and in the intimate flow of creation we find our way back into a new identity and a new name. Christian liturgy has not often tapped that creativity. It has become an affair of the head and an exclusive search for ancient sources. But sexuality that is transformed by love is deeper than our deepest pain, and its energy can flow into the service of God. It is one of the sources of our creativity but, if we banish it, it will simply become one of the dark angels of hell beating again at the gates of our lives. If we love it into life and adoration, it will become a means of healing ourselves and the world's pain. With it we reclothe

the dream. Human personality is a sacrament. We become a sacrament of love.

1. See William Willimon, *Worship as Pastoral Care* (Abingdon 1979) and Michael Marshall, *Renewal in Worship* (Marshall, Morgan & Scott 1982).
2. Sara Maitland, *A Map of the New Country: Women and Christianity* (Routledge 1983), p. 189. See also the whole of chapter 6: 'Language and Spirituality'.
3. Keith Watkins, *Faithful and Fair* (Abingdon 1981), p. 15.
4. C. G. Jung, *Collected Works*, vol. 11 (Routledge 1958), p. 189.
5. See Jim Cotter, *Prayer at Night* (3rd edition 1986; available from 185 Topsham Road, Exeter EX2 6AN and 197 Piccadilly, London W1V 9LF. There is also a companion book: *Prayer in the Day*).
6. Nancy Smith, 'For Every Woman' (unpublished meditation).
7. Anthony Stevens, *Archetype* (Routledge 1982), p. 201.
8. Alternative Service Book, 'Marriage', p. 288.
9. Book of Common Prayer (1662), 'Introduction to the Form of Solemnization of Matrimony'.
10. *Covenant of Friendship* (available from G. C. M., BM 6914, London WC1N 3XX).
11. H. Caffarel, *The Body at Prayer* (SPCK 1978), p. 5.
12. Meinrad Craighead OSB in *Studia Nuptica*, vol. 1, no. 1 (Spring 1978), p. 21.

8

Two Soul Faces

The word of God ... cuts like any double-edged sword but more finely ... (Letter to the Hebrews)

It had been a very difficult ecumenical weekend with a lot of pain expressed. The conference centre had echoed with screams of anger about the status of women within the Church. Some of the men had retreated inside themselves; others were frustrated and angry. It had been tough, connecting up what was going on with the Christian tradition. I had sat up until 3 a.m. on the Sunday morning, wondering how I could preach at the Eucharist the following day. In the end, this is what I said. It is not meant to be a good example of a sermon, but it illustrates what I have to say about preaching and pastoral care.

The hospital room was dark. In it a young man was dying; he was paralysed from the waist downwards. In addition to his multiple injuries, he had developed gangrenous peritonitis, which gives off the most awful stench.

The surgeon who was responsible for his care had asked a young woman technician in the hospital to visit him. She made her way gingerly along the corridor, pushed open the door, reeled back hit by the stench. She tore off down the corridor.

As she ran, she bumped into the surgeon. He smiled. 'So you've seen my man?' Breathless, she stammered, 'No ... the smell ... I couldn't ... I can't.'

The surgeon took her gently by the arm and led her back down the corridor. As they walked, he said to her, 'Look that man needs you. He has lost all sense of worth, of value. Go and discover the man in the stinking darkness.'

She went in, sat by the man, sustained by the surgeon's words. She went back day after day. She was there when he died eight days later.

About three weeks after that, she was still reflecting on her experience. Some words suddenly came to mind:

> All that came to be had life in him,
> and that life was the light of people,
> a light that shines in the dark,
> a light that darkness could not overpower.
>
> (John 1: 4–5)

The penny dropped. Those words suddenly lit up her experience. She found Jesus in a new way for he, too, had entered the stinking darkness.

Jesus had shared the conflicts of being human. He had shared the most profound dejection and rejection. He had met in the depths of himself that darkness that threatens our tentative plans for unity. He had received the projections and the shadows. Whatever conflict, loss of unity, loneliness or rejection we experience, Jesus has been there before. He is, in fact, the most assailed person of all, for he has suffered the worst anxiety: that in the godless depths of our world there is nothing and nothing and nothingness. All unity is shattered, chaos reigns. He is there even when God seems to have abandoned us to our mutual violence. He is there because God is in the stinking darkness. He is the person in the stinking darkness.

That is the vocation to which we are called. Like Jacob we struggle with the conflicts inside and outside, but even when wounded we are called into the dawn. Our vocation is to share the conflict and the pain: if like Jacob we had a ladder with which to climb into heaven, what would we see when we come face to face with God? We would be face to face with the Wounded One, to whom all creation gives worth.

But we are not left alone with the conflict of our humanity. As he beckons gently, 'Discover the man in the stinking darkness,' he clothes us for the struggle with the powers of violence. He stands beside us and takes us by the arm. He offers to clothe us with the vulnerability of love, integrity and hope. The invitation is to trust in a grace that is amazing because that alone can heal our conflicts and renew our hearts. We are clothed to be God's protest against the darkness. You are the community of resurrection, shattered, broken, hurt, but recreated in this great act of unity and reconciliation. Become who you are.

He clothes you now with the wonder of wonders of divine love: at the end of all our exploring . . . at the end of the facing of conflict . . . at the end of entering the darkness . . . we come to acknowledge and celebrate the unity that really matters: 'All is one and one is all in God.'

Preaching is part of 'the paradox of worship'.[1] God works within us in worship, but that does not absolve us from the responsibility of making our response. If God did not take the initiative towards us, we would not be able to make a response. It is what I have described in chapter 1 as 'the mutual giving and receiving of worth', and preaching is part of that. It is not a means to an end. Preaching is not about making better-informed Christians; it is not a tool of teaching; it is not about ethical instruction. It is not a means to anything. It is part of the essence of worship. If we yield to temptations like, 'Preaching is helping people to understand the Bible better,' or, 'Preaching is about converting people to Christ,' we are denying the divine possibilities in people. Preaching is part of the essence of worship because worship enables us to be our true selves available to God for the transformation of the world. Preaching will fail to be worship if it is understood as a means to an end. It is a telling-out of the initiative of God and a clue to our response and responsibility:

> Our liturgical action must help us to see the everyday world transformed; the world of industry, commerce, homes, politics local and national, and so on. Worship may take us out of the world for a time. Jesus often went apart from the world for a time, for prayers and peace. But he went apart with the very intention of returning to the attack with renewed strength and vigour.   (Eric James)[2]

Preaching cares for us when it holds us in that double move-ment and refuses to let us off the paradox.

That understanding of preaching seems to have some important implications for the practice of theology. The basis of theology is the experience of God active in the world. The practice of theology is the reflection upon the self-revealing activity of God. That suggests that one of the best places to begin to do theology is with our personal experience. Those who risk preaching need to develop a theological sensitivity towards the concerns of the world and everyday experience. That seems to be consistent with the development of doctrine and worship historically. The Church has continually reflected upon its experience of God in Christ and it has become a process of reinterpretation. Theological discernment at its best has been about uncovering the values that lie within human experience, personal and corporate, and testing those values against our received traditions.

This is a skill to be acquired not only by a small elite. It is part of the internal dialogue of every preacher and is the life blood of the Christian Church. It is the struggle to discern God and our response to his presence in the ambiguous thrust of everyday events. It may begin, therefore, with a story or parable like the beginning of the sermon in this chapter. The power of that story is about faith and life coming together around a statement about incarnation. But its greater power is that the woman's experience was incarnational. She discovered God-in-Christ within her experience. An interior dialogue had started which helped her to act differently, for she had begun to possess a theology which she could own for herself. Theology is not an amassed body of knowledge to be passed like a parcel from those who know to those who don't know (see also chapters 2 and 4). It is a shared reflection about God's disclosure of himself in Jesus now. That reflection needs to be tested against biblical and doctrinal 'norms', but it can be tested only after it has been experienced.

This seems to be of considerable significance for pastoral care because it says a great deal about how we treat each other. A lot of theology arises from anxiety, anxiety in the face of the unknown. It becomes, consequently, an anxious pursuit for right answers as we stand in front of the unknown attempting to control and manipulate it. That same mode of behaviour can subtly influence preaching. A model of knowledge based on anxiety can lead preachers into being superior people who know it all.

But there is another view of knowledge which is quickly gaining ground in many disciplines. It recognises that the more we know, the more we do not know. Knowledge is a mystery opening before us in which there is always more to learn. There is a wonder in knowledge which can lead to a very different view of each other. Authority, instead of being a domination of others, becomes a shared delight in common discovery. The Greek word for authority, *ex-ousia*, means 'out of being'. When preaching is out of being, it can delight in a common journey together. Preaching can always happen when the soul has two faces: an honesty about the Gospel and an honesty in the face of our questions. I think that this is the way to prevent congregations being simply passive. When they can respond: 'Yes, I find myself in your words because your words come from the depths of human experience and, therefore, are not just yours but also mine . . .,' they have left behind every possibility of being passive. Preaching has become an expression of our solidarity with others. It is an act of pastoral care:

> What does it mean to be a minister in our contemporary society? The image of the wounded healer . . . after all attempts to articulate the predicament of modern man, the necessity to articulate the predicament of the minister himself became the most important. For the minister is called to recognise the sufferings of his time in his own heart and make that recognition the starting point of his service. Whether he tries to enter into a dislocated world, relate to a convulsive generation, or speak to a dying man, his service will not be perceived as authentic unless it comes from a heart wounded by the suffering about which he speaks.   (Henri Nouwen)[3]

If pastoral care can happen when a minister of the Word really connects biblical and theological truth with real human experience, it follows that effective preaching depends on the minister's capacity to know where people are and to speak to that place. Preaching will become part of the dynamic paradox of worship only if it mediates worth from and to

God. That raises two immediate issues about the preacher. The activity of preaching is never a means of seeking approval or having one's vocation justified. It is, therefore, rooted in the experience of being justified by faith. Part of the integrity of preaching is a trusting confidence in my acceptance by God. 'Accept that you are accepted' is every preacher's imperative. The second issue is also about integrity. A true leader will be convinced of unimaginable capacities in others to find their way to the truth. She or he will believe that a congregation has the capacity for a new response to God. They will believe in transformation. For preaching not only depends on the capacity of the preacher to enter the deepest paradoxes of human life; it also depends on the imaginative capacity to grasp the potentiality of that same life.

The hazards on the way to such a view of preaching must be self-evident. The Reformation gave the Bible back to the people, but clergymen made sure they grabbed it back fast! The risk of preachers becoming the sole and authoritarian dispensers of the word of God are all too apparent. That in turn fixes lay people in a limited set of responses: 'I agree,' 'I disagree.' It perpetuates inappropriate authority structures for the people of God. But I believe that preaching which is informed by the insights of pastoral care and set within a context of biblical reflection can be radically different. It can become a moment of disclosure in a struggle to discern God's will and worth within human life.

Preaching is an act of proclamation by the word. Pastoral care is an act of proclamation by presence. In both encounters the gospel of love may be proclaimed and the inexhaustible power of love communicated. The structure of both encounters is remarkably similar. Most sermons have a four-fold structure which is close to what is happening in pastoral care: (i) the identification of the issue; (ii) a reconstruction of that issue; (iii) theological diagnosis and reflection upon it; (iv) pastoral interventions and initiatives resulting from the reflection. Dr Berger, who lectures in pastoral psychology at the University of Nymegen, has highlighted the value of identifying such a structure:

The pattern of counselling can clarify the processes which occur when a person listens to a good sermon. What is the point of seeking for such a pattern? . . . If a pattern clarifies certain processes it gives us the opportunity of discovering and correcting certain flaws that may well block the success of the sermon and make it fruitless if not positively harmful.[4]

Within that structure there is a process which applies equally to preaching and pastoral care. It is the process of accurate empathy. Let me give an example. I was working once with a group of Anglican lay readers around a question of preaching at funerals. I had given them a task to do. They had to prepare a sermon for a particular pastoral situation. None of their sermons engaged me. I was bored, distracted, switched off by them. I didn't feel that any of their sermons were real communications. So I challenged them: 'Tell me about what happened to you last time death happened in your life.' Each spoke deeply, hesitantly, sometimes haltingly about their emotional and spiritual experience of death. 'Now', I said, 'you're communicating something to me.' By getting in touch with their own feelings, they began to put me in touch with mine.

The process of accurate empathy is as relevant to the preacher as to the counsellor. It demands two qualities: The capacity to step into the shoes of another person and feel the world as they feel it and the ability to handle one's own feelings. This quality of empathy is relevant to all preaching, but it is especially demanded at key turning points in life, such as baptisms, funerals, weddings, memorial services and Remembrance Day. The preacher needs to feel empathy with a congregation and to be able to put those feelings into words, relating them to the reality of God. By putting others accurately in touch with what is happening to them, the way is open for the Holy Spirit to work for transformation. People are being opened up in the depths of themselves to the presence of God. When a preacher loses contact with the listeners, they have lost contact with themselves. Stagnation inside the minister quickly damages a congregation, thus growth in a preacher's own life must be a condition for growth in the life of the congregation.

There are other characteristics of pastoral care which could helpfully influence preaching. Authenticity is one of them. This is nowhere better expressed than in one of the seminal books of the twentieth century, *The True Wilderness* by Harry Williams:

> I resolved that I would not preach about any aspect of Christian belief unless it had become part of my own life-blood. For I realised that the Christian truth that I tried to proclaim would speak to those who listened only to the degree in which it was an expression of my own identity.[5]

His identity, that resulted from breakdown and psycho-analysis, demanded that words and self came into a more complete whole. It was the logical conclusion of belief in an incarnate God: 'the Word was made flesh'. Preachers are not like secondhand-furniture dealers passing on secondhand dogmas. Preaching can only be a sharing of a gospel that is true to your experience of yourself and God. Anything less than that is a violation of the paradox of worship.

One further word will illustrate what I am saying about the mutual relationship of preaching and pastoral care. It is the word 'genuineness'. Those who lead worship run the risk of becoming performers. As I said in chapter 5, Christian worship is a great dramatic art. It is the drama of the death and resurrection of Christ. But the Christian drama is not like Greek drama. It does not need any masks. We are who we are.

At the end of St John's Gospel there is a fascinating exploration of this. The gospel begins with a celebration of an incarnate God and it ends with a story about what that means. When Thomas asks to see the scars of Jesus he is not asking for proof that Jesus is risen. He is asking for an assurance that Jesus really had been human, that he hadn't been an illusion, that he hadn't worn a mask of humanity. If Jesus was human *and* risen then there was real hope for humanity. Our scars are important sources of hope for others. They are part of our authenticity in preaching.

But having said that, I believe we should also recognise the important function that roles play in the conduct of worship. We perform roles for the sake of others. If leading worship is the expression of love, we shall need to stay in

roles so that others can feel free. The proper living in a role
is not the same as the wearing of false masks. As we trust
that God knows who we are, we can mediate that God to
others through our roles as priests, preachers and pastors.

Both in the internal process and the external structure of the
pastoral care relationship there are very important parallels
with preaching. I want to return briefly to the external structure and spell out a little more fully what I mean. The sermon
at the beginning of this chapter identifies a problem through
a story. It was a problem within the community in which this
particular sermon happened. The sermon then attempts, and
this is possibly its greatest weakness in terms of craft, to
reconstruct that problem. The end of the story, with its radical
reversal of perspective, achieves that to some degree. The
power of this story lies in its implicit communication of some
of the feelings and struggles within the people concerned.
What follows is a theological reflection based on an understanding of the incarnate God. It links the human story to a
way of understanding how God is in the world. The last part
of the sermon deals both with the pastoral imperative and
the resources needed to fulfil it. To analyse a sermon in this
way is to strip it of some of its mysterious power but it
does enable us to discover a truth in both pastoral care and
preaching. The truth is that by participating in the conflict
and perplexity of another person we can reunderstand the
power of the gospel, which underlines the essential inter-
connectedness of pastoral care and preaching. It is very
difficult to preach from outside the life of a community, so
the structure of a sermon becomes in a sense a vignette of a
continuing pastoral strategy.

I have tried to demonstrate throughout this book that
worship is an activity which engages the whole person.
Contemporary scientific research has helped us understand
more fully the activity of both sides of the brain. The left side
controls the analytical, logical and reflective side of human
life. The right side engages the imaginative, affective, creative
side of us. A friend of mine had a stroke. The doctors were
fascinated that it had happened in the right side of the brain;
most strokes happen on the left side. She is a highly imagin-

ative art therapist. The stress in her life was focussed on the opposite side to most people. This seems to be of relevance to preaching, for if it is to be part of the essence of worship, and not a means to an end, it will need to engage both sides of the brain. Most preaching is very left wing! It appeals to logical people who think in sequences. Whole preaching will not deny our intellectual capacities but it will also draw on story, image, colour, symbols and visual aids to engage the whole of us. Walter Wink underlines the importance of this in the process of Christian nurture:

> I want to see people transformed, which means, practically speaking, that new ideas about the text are not enough. We must get our whole selves involved with it, right brain as well, and struggle to let it endow us with a fuller share of our available humanity . . . We must find ways to bring our whole selves to texts that are themselves the product of processes that involve both hemispheres.[6]

It could be argued that this puts too great a burden on what in many churches is now a ten-minute discourse. There is some truth in that, although it may only highlight the fact that we expect too much of sermons anyway. Most preaching would be far more effective if it happened in the context of a growing and learning community. One of the effects of secularisation in the Western world is to make Christian faith more clearly a matter of choice but, far from undermining the fabric of real Christian living, secularisation could strengthen it. As Christian faith becomes a matter of choice, adult Christians will demand more resources for growing in faith and action. Ten-minute sermons will not nourish people for the rigorous demands of discipleship. Many patterns will develop according to the needs of different local communities, but the American episcopalian pattern has much to commend it. In many such churches congregations spend part of the eucharistic ministry of the Word in smaller groups following all kinds of experimental forms of learning, often designed for particular age-groups. The sermon is part of an educational process aimed at helping people to discover what God wants them to be in the middle of the ambiguous paradoxes of life where questions are posed at their sharpest.

There is one final dimension that pastoral care brings to the practice of preaching. In a pastoral relationship there often comes a time when the person caring becomes convinced that some issue is being avoided or some area of darkness ignored. A moment of confrontation comes, in which the carer tries to bring that to light. The person being counselled may bring the question up but in the last three minutes of the session when it feels safe that nothing will happen. There is little doubt that a similar sort of phenomenon can arise in congregations. Community conflicts, divisions over issues of principle, pastoral neglect, apathy about the gospel can all begin to erode a congregation's vitality. There are times when preaching needs to bring to light what darkness holds. As long as the minister can recognise her or his collusion with this darkness, there is some chance of a confrontation in love. In pastoral care confrontation does not normally happen until a relationship of trust is established. The same is normally true in preaching, although I have known the rare occasion when an outsider was able to speak a word of truth, which led to a congregation being transformed. Because preaching is an activity of the Kingdom of God, it will be an instrument to remind us that the Church is a foretaste of God's intention for the whole of humanity and that anything in its life which militates against that is an offence to the purposes of God. There is a large measure of cultural discrimination in the Christian church, and sermons must find ways of cutting through conventional ideas and patterns of behaviour.

It is part of the history of the Christian Church that the Holy Spirit gives flashes of insight to people. They have seen the ordinary in a new way, transformed, and they see 'the dearest freshness deep down things' (Gerard Manley Hopkins). Preaching is one way people can be renewed, seeing the freshness of God in the everyday; that opens up the possibility of hope and new life. Occasionally it may completely transform the life of an individual and lead them to turn right round and face the future. The soul has at least two faces. It can apprehend in two modes at the same time. It can apprehend God and it can apprehend all that it means to be human. Preachers are those who live with the conscious recognition that their soul has two faces. When that consciousness exists and is acted on, they become the servants of compassion.

1. I am indebted for this phrase to Michael Perry. It is the title of his book, *The Paradox of Worship* (SPCK 1977).
2. Eric James, *The Roots of the Liturgy* (Prism Pamphlet, no. 1, 1962), p. 7.
3. Henri Nouwen, *The Wounded Healer* (Doubleday 1982), p 4.
4. W. Berger, 'Preaching and Counselling' in *Tydsschrift voor Pastorale Psychologie*, vol. 4, no. 2 (June 1972).
5. Harry Williams, *The True Wilderness* (Constable 1965), p. 8.
6. Walter Wink, *Transforming Bible Study* (SCM 1981), p. 32.

9

Fragile People

The parson boomed like a dockyard gun at a christening.
Somebody read from the bible. It seemed hours.
I got the feeling you were curled up inside the box, listening.
There was the thud of hymn-books, the stench of flowers.

(CHARLES CAUSLEY)

A friend exploded into my home one morning. 'That was an absolutely dreadful induction last night,' she said. 'I just hope the new vicar didn't see what was going on. It would have ruined the whole event for him.' 'What on earth happened?' I responded. 'That bishop . . . that bloody bishop . . . all he did throughout the service was to fidget, look around . . . and every five minutes he checked his watch. It was unbelievable; completely wrecked the liturgy for me.'

It would be easy to dismiss that as an over-sensitive reaction to a minor matter. But perhaps it helps us face up to a serious issue. Liturgy is often experienced very differently in the pew than it is in the sanctuary of the pulpit. Elizabeth's reaction leaves us in no doubt as to the value and significance she was giving to that liturgical event. Because of the peculiar jobs that I have had over the last ten years I have also spent a great deal more time than most clergy in the pew. It is a privileged place from which to reflect on the conduct of liturgy and those who conduct it. My experience has not been exhilarating. I could count on one hand the number of times when I have felt really cared for in a liturgy. But that is not my major concern. What disturbs me much more is the deadness, sloppiness, lack of preparation and any sense of making connections which characterise the leadership of so much worship. It has felt too often like a nod towards the absence of God. Why, I kept on asking, are sermons so badly prepared, when numerous lay people tell me in the course of my work that they are longing for connections to be made between their life experience and biblical tradition? Why do some clergy slouch around the altar or alternatively walk around as if God was a regimental sergeant-major barking his orders? Why do clergy, servers, choir appear in tatty, and sometimes dirty, linen? Why do some bend over backwards to assure us apparently that nothing of very great significance is happening? Why are the intercessions so poorly constructed, so sterile and repetitive, so devoid of empathy and raw human need and real human passion?

Those who sit in the pew do not miss these things and, like Elizabeth, are baffled as to why priests (and bishops!) invest so much time and energy in so many other activities and give so little time to the conduct of corporate worship. In her particular instance time seemed to be grudged in what was almost certainly an over busy life. Some clergy, mercifully, share this sense of bewilderment and are puzzled at their own lack of investment in the leadership of corporate worship. Some of that mutual bafflement can be accounted for by the crisis in ritual in British post-Christian society. It can also be put down to a growing lack of confidence in the power of liturgy to achieve the sustaining and healing of people. Theological colleges and seminaries can take some of the responsibility because of their inability to make creative worship a credible part of the syllabus. In 1983 I heard of one Anglican theological college in which no member of staff took any responsibility for the worship and liturgy of the college and where worship featured only as part of the traditional syllabus with a heavy emphasis on its history. This is often paralleled in the wider church.

The problem is a multi-faceted one, and one cannot pretend there are simple diagnoses or solutions. I am convinced that one reason for the deadness in so much liturgical leadership is the over-busyness of clergy. I have known at first hand more than once the terrible toll in physical and emotional health that the cruel Church can exact from its servants. Exhaustion, lassitude and mental inertia are not good ingredients for lively liturgy. But, more importantly, there is something peculiarly distracting about over-busyness. It leads to physical postures and mental attitudes that are disconnected. There is no real syncronicity between the liturgical act and those leading it. Like the bishop, clergy sometimes seem to be checking their watches every five minutes!

A further source of difficulty is the loss of identity in many clergy. Paul Pruyser highlights this problem with particular reference to the notion of 'blessing':

> When worship leaders perform sloppily in their liturgical work, they are obviously not attributing a high professional value to this part of their activities. And when they perform badly in benediction, the unspoken messages to the congregation are that: (1) benedictions are rather meaningless, (2) the pastor does not deem the people worthy of receiving them, (3) the pastor himself has long given up thought of providence, or (4) the pastor refuses to shoulder the shepherd's role.[1]

Pruyser suggests that there is a connection between the priest's identification of his or her role and the notion of authorisation from the community. If ordination is the way in which a church orders the life of its community, then formal priesthood is the authorisation to ensure that the life of the community goes on. In one sense it can be about doing nothing. It is simply the gift to bring a community into being so that it fulfils its role in the world. If a priest doubts that she or he has been given that authorisation the community is demeaned, because it is that community that has made the priest the primary instrument of the action and response of the people of God in worship. If a priest fails to be a window into that action and response, the faith and adoration of the community may be impoverished. The presence of the priest provides coherence for the community to fulfil God's purposes in the world. That is why both sexes need to be priests: the community of Christ is the foretaste of one human community in which women and men take coequal responsibility for the life of humanity and creation: Vincent Donovan writes of his experience with the Masai in East Africa:

> And that man who called the community together and held it together; at the end of the instructions he would not be the one in the community who knew the most theology,

.the theologian. He would not be the preacher or the evan-
gelist of the community. He would not be the prophet. He
would not be the most important member in the
community, in the sense of being the one who was to make
the most important contribution, of which the community
might someday be capable.

But he would be the focal point of the whole community,
the one who would enable the community to act, whether
in worship or in service.[2]

This experience in two radically different cultures, the U.S.A.
and East Africa, reveals a remarkable degree of syncronicity.
Both are agreed that at the core of the experience of those who
lead worship, the priests, is the community's authorisation to
enable it to act in love and adoration. I shall return later in
the chapter to the implications of that.

A third factor in this crisis of deadness is the projections
issue. Those who are pastors and leaders of worship are on
the receiving end of a whole range of projections. They are
expected to be idealisations of goodness and holiness. I think
that this can be best illustrated by something that happened
when a priest announced that he was leaving for another
parish and there would be no replacement. There was tremendous anxiety. The anxiety was not, surprisingly, about not
having another priest. It was about the fact that there
wouldn't be a family living in the vicarage anymore. The
village needed the vicarage family to keep its idealised image
of family life intact.

Projections on to clergy will vary in different social and
cultural contexts, but they operate because people sometimes
need us to be something other than what we are. In an inner
urban deanery synod I was once shouted down because I
would not collude with the notion that a priest was a father-
figure six feet above contradiction. If we allow others to tell
us what we should do, I argued, we shall in fact deprive
ourselves of that glorious responsibility for ourselves, our
neighbour and our creation, all of which is the handiwork of
God. We always have a choice. We can collude with the
projections, as numerous clergy do, or we can grow in self-
awareness and commitment to the growth of others. This
problem of projections becomes most acute in liturgy, because

it is there that the priest is most exposed, though it would be very different for both women and men if a woman was in focus. The projections game prevents people from owning both their own goodness and their own darkness. I have known, as a priest in a team of lay people, how easy it was for my colleagues to invest me with a kind of super-goodness and so deny themselves the possibility of having it.

Over-busyness, loss of identity and the projections game are all part of this multi-faceted problem of why so many of those who lead worship are baffled by their lack of investment in it. But these still do not add up to a complete answer. Complete answers are, anyway, strangely elusive. But these factors still leave me discontented. So I pursue the question, why? I have become increasingly convinced that one of the root causes of the deadness lies in the loss of any real conviction about justification by faith. One clerical oddity is an almost compulsive need to keep God in business. There is a good deal of paternal/maternalism and showmanship in priesthood. One of its consequences is to take over the liturgy from God and to manipulate his presence. The end result feels more like the absence of God. But underlying that need to rest in paternal/maternalism or to indulge in charismatic showmanship is an agnosticism about our own worth before God. I grow increasingly convinced that justification by faith alone challenges two of the greatest sicknesses in the Church today: the compulsive over-busyness of clergy and the timid disobedience of numerous lay people to fulfil the challenge of their baptism. Both are symptoms of a lack of real worth. They are in fact disclosures of self-hatred. If self-hatred is sharply in focus in the liturgy it is no wonder that the whole business seems dead.

This brings me to the issue of integrity. I wrote earlier (see chapter 8) about the nature of doing theology and connecting real-life experience with biblical and theological truth. Many clergy are the victims of a theological process in which no real attention has been paid to the connections. It is a costly business because human experience does not easily fit much received theological tradition. But my work with lay people for the last ten years has taught me that one of the most exciting explorations is the mutual exposure of human and biblical experience. People connect inside themselves and then begin to act on that connectedness in the social and political world. Few clergy seem to have experienced that same excitement and so come across to many lay people as disconnected. Sermons lack vitality, intercessions seem narrow and lifeless. Clergy are ignored when it comes to the struggle with the sharp questions and ethical dilemmas at the other end of the commuter line or in the struggles of the local community. Theological education urgently needs to find a new style. A Methodist minister expressed this strikingly:

> Our children learn and worship through something like the 'Partners in Learning' scheme, geared to person-centred learning. Their views and communication, in response to the material presented, is the basis of what follows the in-put. At the moment they are expected to make the transition from that to permanently listening to what *someone else* thinks. However skilled and learned the preacher is, this is not their way. *We* have helped it not to be.[3]

We should expect those responsible for theological education to be at the sharp end of these questions. The truth more often seems to be that they are manufacturing theological and ecclesiastical masks for future clergy to wear. Those who suffer are the millions of lay people who expect much and receive little. I suspect that underneath the masks there is much bitter suffering too.

I have called this phenomenon, fragility. I use that word because most fragile things are usually very beautiful and there is a beauty in priesthood, even if it is the savage beauty of the suffering servant in Isaiah, chapters 52 and 53. But there is another kind of fragility, and it belongs to our twentieth-century dilemma about worship. It is powerfully expressed by the Welsh poet, Harri Webb, in his poem 'Cilmeri':

> Here is only stone, water and death.
> In a dead season. There is no guarantee
> That anything will come of this: no sacrament
> is valid any more.[4]

Obviously I am not able to go all the way with Harri Webb although he expresses how it feels for many people. But I do think that he has got close to an element within the paradox

of worship: 'There is no guarantee that anything will come
of this.' It is part of the peculiar nature of worship that it
offers no guarantees, no assurances, that it will make any
difference at all. *Worship is in that sense the supreme act of faith.*
It is an obedient response to the conviction that in the end
light will bring out all that darkness holds. On the day I
wrote this 500 bodies were dug up in a Buenos Aires cemetery,
each with a bullet-hole through the head. All the prayers
that had been offered up against violence and oppression
contained no guarantee that anything would happen. In the
end the hope is that violence will be exposed and the
oppressor brought to the place of justice. Those who lead
worship have to live with the uneasy conviction that it offers
no guarantees that anything will be changed.

If that is so, our worship will only be alive if we find some
other meaning in it. Carl Jung suggested two ways through:
(a) that worship enables us to get in touch with the depths
of human experience; and (b) that it protects us from being
overwhelmed by those depths by containing us within a
patterned ritual. We have to discover ways of dealing with
the depths of ourselves without destroying ourselves. Liturgy
is a protection against the darkness and a screen on which
we show pictures of God's purposes for the future of humanity
and creation. The overwhelming experience is perhaps felt
most of all in relation to God. We desire him but we also
want to flee from him. That experience is expressed again
and again in the book of Psalms. In worship we contain the
loss of guarantees. We contain some of the forces that struggle
in the depths of our being. In worship we attempt:

> to encounter our darkness and our light:
> And then at last we shall be whole.[5]

Those who lead worship have, therefore, the burdened privilege of creating those conditions in which the intolerable can
be contained, especially the intolerable prospect that 'there
is no guarantee that anything will come of this'. Worship
pitches us headlong into a real struggle about doubt and faith.
The protection against that struggle overwhelming those who
lead worship is the authorisation that what they do is on
behalf of the whole Church and is not dependent on individual
needs and feelings. C. S. Lewis warned against the dangers

of allowing personal feelings full play in ritual: 'The modern habit of doing ceremonial things unceremoniously is no proof of humanity; rather it proves the offender's inability to forget himself in the rite, and his readiness to spoil for everyone else the proper pleasure of ritual.'

I want to suggest six measures that can be taken by those who lead worship and which might help to alleviate some of these difficulties. However, they do not let us off the hook of living with the paradoxes of worship:

1. Those who enable others to worship need to be still. The great problem about the bishop mentioned at the beginning of this chapter was that throughout the liturgy he was never still. To be still at the centre of our being is no easy task. It is a skill that has to be fought for and continually relearnt. But some very simple rules would aid us in the attempt to achieve it in liturgy. The situation in most vestries prior to an act of worship is very disturbing. Servers fuss around. Choirboys turn up late and choirladies fuss around them like mother hens. Organists come unprepared and argue with clergy about tunes. The whole situation requires some simple discipline. All those responsible should be ready fifteen minutes before the act of worship is due to begin. In the clergy vestry there could be a ten-minute rule of silence before the service. By that time all clergy would be robed and ready. They could be still themselves and begin to prepare for worship. I am not suggesting that simple rules make all the difference in the world. They do not, because being truly still in the centre of our life only comes through disciplined meditation learnt over years of practice. But these simple devices would create a climate in which we could reclaim that experience for ourselves and others. Free Church ministers may need to resist the temptation to fill the space with long extempore prayers, which can also be a defence against enjoying the silence of God.

2. Clergy and lay people need to recognise the crisis of integrity within their common experience. By integrity I mean the business of 'only connect'; of really linking up and integrating

the life of faith with the raw material of everyday human existence. There is a growing interest in the world Church in theological education by extension, some of which is based on the educational model of experience–reflection–action–experience . . . It is a cyclical model in which we learn to reflect on historical traditions and act according to our insights. Our actions bring new experience and so the cycle begins again. (See also chapters 2 and 4.) Many congregations could ensure that some of the community begin to develop these skills so that the whole community could move towards a much more integrated faith. Many lay people are resistant to clergy sharing in that exploration because, as one person put it, 'Nothing will kill exploration faster than a clergyman on the journey with you.' Nevertheless, the need is so urgent that some measures need to be taken. In-service training in all the churches might also make the task of theological reflection and interpretation high on its agenda. The British churches could learn a great deal about theological education by extension, especially from the Latin American church. That struggle for integrity is one of the foundation stones of good worship.

3. We need to free ourselves from the mentality that worship is something that 'just happens'. Like all great art it is born out of the toughest discipline. I recall an interview with Robin Cousins, the ice dancer, when he told how he had achieved success. He had lived in a grotty bed-sitter in Notting Hill Gate in London and had got up to practise every morning at 5 a.m. Then he had done a low-paid job so that he could be back at the ice rink by 4 p.m. to put in four hours more practice. Michael Marshall draws on a different analogy to make the same point:

> Like a good batsman the eye, the body and the mind must all be saying the same thing, each bringing a discipline to bear upon all the others, if the batsman is to achieve the best stroke with, seemingly, the least self-conscious effort.[6]

Those analogies both underline the importance of learning disciplined skills in worship. Those who lead worship do not need to have all the skills but they do need to ensure that the skills are acquired within the congregation.

4. I have treasured the dream with which this book began, because it gave me one powerful insight into the nature of worship. If you want to see God today you have to bend very low, as low as the poor stranger who sits at the door and asks why the land is burnt. Franz Kafka drew a parallel picture:

> And if I were to cast myself down before you and weep and tell you, what more would you know about me than you know about hell when someone tells you it is hot and dreadful? For that reason alone we human beings ought to stand before one another as reverently, as reflectively, as lovingly, as we would before the entrance to hell.[7]

There is an essential quality of humility in the leadership of worship, which means having a rigorous grasp of one's own limitations. Humility is not a skill to be learnt but a way of being open to risk. It means expressing one's own needs clearly and making a congregation aware of the ways in which it can develop other areas which are required for good liturgy. That implies being ready to sit back and enjoy others' abilities and skills, which I can never possess and must not manipulate for my own ends. An essential element in any teamwork is the mutual enjoyment of each other. One of the great tensions in many congregations will inevitably be between the development of charismatic ministries and the ordering of them. But that is part of the paradox of the Church: there will always be a struggle between the individual and the corporate.

5. There is a need for a massive change of consciousness within most of the major denominations about the place of representative ministry. Bishops, priests and deacons have all been over-valued to the detriment of the apostolate, the priesthood and the diaconate of the whole Body of Christ. We have lost sight of the fact that the authorised ministries are signs by which we recognise Christ's gifts in the whole Body. That is not to devalue authorisation or ordination, both of which are important for the ordering of the whole Body; it is setting them in a proper context. Vincent Donovan again picks up this theme with reference to priesthood in the Masai tribes:

> In that one supreme moment in his life when Jesus did offer sacrifice once and for all, he gathered into himself the

whole meaning of priesthood and sacrifice, and obliterated forever the need of a priestly caste. The result of that action and his entirely original contribution was, for the first time in the history of religion, to enable an entire people to be priests. Is this not one of the biggest differences between Christianity and all other religions on the face of the earth?[8]

I have insisted throughout this book that liturgy is the work of the whole people of God. That places those who lead worship in a position of burdened privilege. Part of their fragility is to recognise that they are authorised to enable the whole Body to intercede before God. They are only special people inasmuch as the local Christian community and the bishop (or equivalent) has authorised them to fulfil that role on the community's behalf. Most Christian congregations are a long way from this vision, and it will require at least another decade of consciousness-raising through lay-training programmes and reformed theological education before we see this vision become a reality. Perhaps those who are most in a position of burdened privilege, the bishops and over-seers, could take a dynamic role in reshaping this vision?

6. At several points in the New Testament, worship and the notion of priesthood seem to be connected (see, e.g., Colossians 1: 15–20; Hebrews 2:10–18; Revelation 5:6–14; John 17; Ephesians 2: 11–22). Some notion of priesthood seems to be at the centre of the worship of most major Christian traditions. In the biblical tradition, and especially in the passages that I have just quoted, there does seem to be a definable double movement which may be a key link between pastoral care and worship and may provide us with precisely that paradigm that will give coherence to this book. The priesthood of Christ is first of all an entering into the depths of all that it means to be human. He is 'the brother'. Christ stands in solidarity with his people as he comes to share life in its heights and depths. There is no cul-de-sac in the whole created universe that has not been visited by the Love made known in this man. Those who lead worship are pastors, who share the lives of those who inhabit many communities. The pastor will not have access to all those communities but they will be penetrated by the priesthood of the whole Body.

But there is another movement to the priesthood of Christ. It is the priestly work and effort of bringing all that life before God. Liturgy is not some pure, untouchable entity handed on for aesthetic pleasure. Nor is it a tickle for the id. It is about heartbreak and yearning, breakdown and expectation. In another place I have written this about the nature of Christ's priesthood:

> We forget too easily that Jesus was a marginal person whom Christians claim took human meaning into the meaning of God. By that action the meaning and value of those who experience themselves on the margins of human society was changed for ever. Life which had taken the brunt of prejudice and discrimination was restored at the centre of God's life . . . the humanity of Jesus . . . will not allow any human being to be devalued without it being an affront to the dignity of God because the humanity of Jesus has made an irreversible difference to God himself.[9]

Priesthood is a sign of ascension, a sign in the here and now that Christ has claimed the whole of human life to its margins and offers it in costly intercession before God. That double movement is, I believe, the coherent thread that draws pastoral care and worship into a single whole.

I have written at length about those who lead worship, not because I over-estimate their importance but because the task of enabling a community to carry the whole of human life into God is a costly business. It is, consequently, very fragile and so are the people who exercise this burdened privilege. That fragility has both negative and positive aspects and I have tried to do justice to both. Nobody captures that fragility better than Dylan Thomas in his poem of resurrection:

> Though they be mad and dead as nails,
> Heads of the characters hammer through daisies;
> Break in the sun till the sun breaks down,
> And death shall have no dominion.[10]

1. Paul Pruyser: 'The Master Hand: Psychological Notes on Pastoral Blessing' in W. B. Oglesby Jr (ed.), *The New Shape of Pastoral Theology: Essays in Honor of Seward Hiltner* (Nashville: Abingdon 1969), p. 361.
2. Vincent Donovan, *Christianity Rediscovered* (SCM 1982), pp. 144–5.
3. Sue Featherstone in a paper for a Methodist Division of Ministries Curriculum Conference.
4. Harri Webb, 'Cilmeri' in *Twelve Modern Anglo-Welsh Poets*, ed. Don Dale-Jones and Randal Jenkins (University of London Press 1975), p. 107.
5. From Michael Tippett's oratorio, 'A Child of Our Time'.
6. Michael Marshall, *Renewal in Worship* (Marshall Morgan & Scott 1982), p. 54.
7. Frank Kafka, 'Letter of 1903' in *Letters to Friends, Family and Editors*, translated by Richard and Clara Winston (John Calder 1979).
8. Vincent Donovan, op. cit., p. 140.
9. Robin Green, 'The Church' in *Prejudice and Pride*, ed. Bruce Galloway (Routledge 1983), pp. 145–6.
10. Dylan Thomas, 'And Death Shall Have No Dominion'.

10

His Story and Ours

'Father, may they be one in us, as you are in me and I am in you.' (ST JOHN'S GOSPEL)

I must now try to draw all the diverse threads of this book together. I want to do that by exploring what it means to be a person and the ways in which the symbols of the Christian tradition can inform that understanding. Those symbols can be apprehended in numerous ways. What I have tried to demonstrate is that there is a key connection between how the symbols are mediated in worship and the growth of people. Worship, by its very nature, cares for people because it creates a matrix within which both our individuality and our sociality can grow.

We live in a fragmented and alienated society in which the myths of individualism and collectivism threaten our unique identity. The legacy of the Enlightenment is the reduction of the person to the individual: this in turn makes relationships with others a problem. But it is even more serious than that: if the person is lost, we are swallowed up into a mass in which we lose our identity and meaning. That is then mirrored in the collectivist vision of human life: Marx, in asserting the priority of the universal, also subjugates people to being ciphers in a meaningless and undifferentiated heap of humanity. As I tried to argue in chapter 1, those involved in the whole field of psychoanalytic psychology and pastoral care and counselling can become trapped in those same myths. There is a whole arena of debate today in the fields of psychology and sociology which the Christian Church needs to enter, because at the moment there are no adequate models being offered which hold together a proper balance of the individual and the universal in our understanding of what it means to be a person.

The exploration of Christian worship and its symbols is able to inform that debate because worship belongs in that arena of human life where there is a confrontation between the conscious and the unconscious. In one of the many debates that formed the background to this book, worship was described by a Norwegian pastor as 'a kind of collective dreaming'. One of the ways in which we deal with the confrontation mentioned above is by dreaming. Carl Jung argues time and again that we are helped towards our 'individuation' by our dreams and our reflections on them. 'Individuation' is that grand design that sums up who we are, helping us towards greater maturity and human awareness. Worship seems to me to be a collective example of that: in worship the individual can be brought into contact with the universal and caught up into a dream of what human life is really all about. I want, therefore, to take four Christian symbols, which I believe not only inform one of the most urgent debates of our time, about who a person is, but also summarise the themes of this book and draw them together into the coherence of Christian orthodoxy.

The first symbol is that of *incarnation*, illustrated by the following story. A Roman Catholic nun had observed an open-heart operation. She had spent most of her ministry in a developing country and was in awe as the surgeon invited her to observe the actual opening of the heart. She described it as a 'moment of intimate vulnerability'. Later on she was struggling to express this experience which, she said, had 'opened up the blood-stream between the human and the divine' in an act of worship. In her own way she was reclaiming the Christian symbol of incarnation to make sense of all the feelings in the operating theatre. Worship makes concrete the connections between our experience of God and our feelings. When she told me this, I was reminded of the one of the most ancient stories in the Jewish scriptures: the story of Jacob's dream: 'He had a dream; a ladder was there, standing on the ground with its top reaching to heaven; and there were angels of God going up it and coming down.'[1] That dream was an important stage in the whole formation of Jacob as a person in his own right: in the later struggle with one of the 'messengers of God' we begin to see the individual and the social brought together in him.[2] Both stories are an early vision of what happens when God and humanity are brought into relationship with each other. The Christian claim is that the supreme expression of that relationship came in the person of Jesus. He is 'the blood-stream between the human and the divine'.

I want now to take three examples of how that can be expressed in worship. The first is drawn from our Jewish inheritance. I was at the Western wall in Jerusalem observing the *barmitzvah* ceremonies, when Jewish boys are initiated both into adulthood and into sharing in the Jewish liturgy. I was struck first of all by the natural spontaneity and fun of the ceremonies. But what also came through very powerfully was the way in which the Jew uses his whole body in the worship of God. The whole person, both as an individual and as part of a corporate history, was to be brought into relation with God. 'You shall love the Lord your God with all your heart, and with all your soul, and with all your mind, and with all your strength.'

The second example came to my mind when I had to bend very low indeed to enter the basilica at Bethlehem. It is part of Catholic practice to make an oblation at the place in the Nicene Creed where the incarnation is celebrated: 'Who for us men, and for our salvation came down from heaven, and was incarnate by the Holy Ghost of the Virgin Mary, and was made man . . .' The extension of the whole body into a posture of humble oblation is an expression of incarnation. It says something about the divine humility and self-emptying, and it also says: 'If you want to find God today, you must bend very low.'

My third example is rather different. So far I have written nothing about the place of music in worship. I value immensely the part that all kinds of music can play in its enrichment, but I cannot sing and so I have to struggle especially hard with the ways in which music can take root in our selves and mediate the presence of God within us. There are various aspects to this. John Eaton in his study of the relation of prophecy and liturgy in the Old Testament highlights the important relationship between the poetry of the prophets and the music of the Jewish liturgy:

We may say then that worship in Israel was characterised
by the word, above all the poetic word; flying on great
wings of imagination, it bore thought and feeling from God
to man and from man to God, making a true communion
of mind and soul.

   The vision, then, that illuminated Israelite worship was
primarily grasped and shared through rapturous poetry,
however much it was supported by music, dancing and
drama.[3]

The power of music lies in its articulation of those parts of
our self that are lost for words. It is an activity of incarnation
because it earths the experience of God in the depths of our
self. It can move us to responding to God even when our
intellect is afflicted with doubt, our will with apathy or our
heart with suffering.

The Christian symbol of incarnation, as it is mediated to
us through worship, is able to hold together the sense of our
own individuality with a more universal vision. It connects
us to others and to God, because it is the symbol through
which we understand that the whole of human experience
has been taken into God, and there is nothing in our experience that is alien from God.

The second symbol is that of *passion*. In chapter 1, I
explored the different ways in which worship is an 'environment' or, as I have described it in this chapter, a 'matrix'.
At many points in the book I have touched on aspects of
human suffering and pain. One of the basic threats to our
humanity is the experience of pain and suffering. The symbol
of the passion of Christ as it is mediated to us through worship
makes it possible for us to set the passion of humanity in a
context of meaning. A great deal of that human passion occurs
at the meeting point of our individuality and sociality. John
Macquarrie summarises that dilemma:

   By his very nature, man must create political and social
   structures and institutions, yet as soon as these have been
   created, they acquire a life of their own; they no longer
   serve human life but tyrannize it and dehumanize it. How
   many millions of people have lived or are even living now
   under regimes that stifle them and make for many a decent
   human life almost impossible?[4]

Reinhold Niebuhr accentuated that when he said: 'The church can be the Anti-Christ and when it denies that possibility it is the Anti-Christ.'

During my time as a parish priest, I have become aware of how powerful this corporate shadow is and how lethal its consequences can be. Christian communities can develop very powerful myths about themselves and one of these is the myth of being 'loving, caring and nice', whilst continuing to act in vicious and destructive ways. The most vulnerable, or the most exposed, members of that community can become the victims of that kind of behaviour. Scapegoating is perhaps the most common way in which Christian communities deal with that repressed 'shadow'. When scapegoating starts, as I know to my own terrible cost, the whole life of a church, including its worship, can be infected.

The only way to deal with that is through the symbol of the 'passion', for the shadow needs to be brought out into the open and to be dealt with for what it really is. Here one of the most powerful expressions of the 'passion' can be brought into play. Christ is the 'Scapegoat'. In that symbol we find focussed all that people most fear and dread. When Christ is lifted up, we are presented with an image of our deepest fears. The biblical picture is that of 'the serpent lifted up in the wilderness' (John 3:13–14). To be faced with Christ the Scapegoat is to enter into the depths of our own darkness. Jim Cotter has prepared a new form of Compline (Night Office) and some of the prayers for it capture this meeting with our own sinister darkness:

> It is an ancient unknown, silent and dark
> But to enter the darkness in trust is to emerge more whole
> To go further into the inner caverns of badness and self-hatred,
> with steadiness and courage, is to emerge into a broad place
> a place of greater honesty and clarity in encounter with others . . .[5]

Worship is an environment of healing because it enables us to face the truth about ourselves. But as Rudolph Otto pointed out again and again, it performs an even more important function than that. It helps us to 'contain' the

depths of human experience so that we can face the unspeak-
able and think the unthinkable. The symbol of the 'passion'
of Christ summarises the implications of God entering into
the human tragedy without shirking in any way the real
power of human darkness. The illustration that I gave of the
parish at the beginning of chapter 6 is a very powerful
example of this.

My third symbol is that of *resurrection*. The resurrection of
Christ is mediated through worship because worship is not
a satisfaction of our immaturity. Christian worship makes
demands on our ability to grow. One of the most moving
moments in my own ministry was at the end of one service
when three people came and told me that they intended to
act differently as the result of a sermon that I had preached.
When worship is an affirmation of the absolute life-fullness
of God, it begins to be a preparation ground for our values
and commitments. At the heart of worship lies the continuing
humanity of the Son of God in the world. So worship is the
preparation for mission: through it our perspectives are
altered and our motivations purified. That is the impact of
worship making the glory of God present. We are once again
at the frontiers of individuality and sociality. As participating
in worship enhances my own sense of individuality, I begin
to discover how that affects my relationship with the worlds
and the neighbours I am daily in touch with. It becomes a
kind of memory in which we learn to write new poetry in our
lives:

> But one must also have been beside the dying, must have
> sat beside the dead in a room with open windows and fitful
> noises. And still it is not yet enough to have memories. . . .
> For the memories themselves are not yet experiences. Only
> when they have turned to blood within us, to glance and
> gesture, nameless and no longer to be distinguished from
> ourselves – only then can it happen that in a most rare
> hour the first word of a poem arises in their midst and goes
> forth from them.   (Rilke)[6]

The final symbol, and the most significant, is that of *Trinity*.
In the Western tradition there are two traditions for talking
about what it means to be a 'person'. I have already discussed
what I believe to be the limitations of the first; the individu-

alism of the Enlightenment collapses into the collectivism of classic Marxism. But there is another view, more subliminal, which has persisted throughout European history. It is what might be described as the trinitarian view of the 'person'. It is impossible to go into all the implications of that history in this particular book, but there has been a growing consensus from many different parts of the Church that the being of God lies in the relation of persons. In God, there is no split between the one and the many, the individual and the universal. In God, the uniqueness of each person is preserved in a way that neither collapses into individualism nor into collectivism. Dr Colin Gunton, in a masterly survey of how trinitarian thinking can illuminate our understanding of the 'person' concludes:

> It is the utter and complete self-giving of the eternal Word, obedient to the Father and dependent upon the Spirit, that makes the particular historic person, Jesus Christ, at the same time the way of the many to God. . . . The world and all in it takes its creation and recreation from the trinitarian relatedness of Father, Son and Spirit.[7]

Worship is inclusive because it contains the whole of human experience which is now included in God. It is, therefore, catholic in the fullest and best sense of that word. But it is inclusive also in a much wider sense: it is inclusive in terms of the whole human race. Liturgy is set free to incorporate the insights and the contributions that come from the worldwide Christian community. The universal relatedness of the Trinity helps us to relate to each other on a worldwide basis. Worship which mediates to us the fullness of life in the Trinity, also helps us come to terms with those ambiguous sides of the divine nature which we find disturbing. Symbols like wrath, fire, water and blood all bring us face to face with realities that we might wish to shy away from. The power of the 'trinitarian' symbol is to include in our human vision and imagination undreamt-of possibilities and opportunities.

But that is always held in tension with something that is just as important. The Symbol of 'Trinity' protects our 'inwardness' and our individuality. As we recognise the universal nature of God, so we are led to the fullest appreciation of our own individuality and uniqueness. There is an intimacy in worship which comes from my own inner self being touched by the beauty of God. As that inner self encounters the universality of God, we are faced with issues of urgent and universal importance for the future of humanity.

Those four symbols – incarnation, passion, resurrection and trinity – summarise all that I have tried to comprehend in beginning to explore a field largely untouched in British pastoral theology. Many of the areas I have focussed on are no more than signposts, pointing to issues and problems that require much more work. In this chapter I have tried to indicate where Christian orthodoxy, liturgy and pastoral care might meet. I have also attempted to highlight the prophetic nature of such an exploration. I am convinced that in the debate which draws on the vast richness of Christian tradition and on contemporary experience, it will be possible to offer a vision to our desperately fragmented and alienated society, which is torn apart daily by politicians who have swallowed the corrupt myths of both individualism and collectivism. By harnessing Jesus' story to ours we might still be saved.

1. Genesis 28:12.
2. Genesis 32:22–9.
3. John Eaton, *Vision in Worship* (SPCK 1981), p. 106.
4. John Macquarrie, *In Search of Humanity* (SCM 1982), p. 92.
5. Jim Cotter, *Prayer at Night* (3rd edition 1986), pp. 64–5. (Available from 185 Topsham Road, Exeter EX2 6AN and 197 Piccadilly, London W1V 9LF.)
6. R. M. Rilke, *Die Aufzeichnungen des Malte Laurids Brigge* (Insel Verlag 1966), p. 124.
7. Colin Gunton, 'The One, the Three and the Many' (Inaugural Lecture at Kings College, London, 1985), p. 13.

Epilogue – Being Here Now

But if only the good God would open my eyes and unseal my ears, so that I might behold the face of my community. (GEORGES BERNANOS)

The scene is one place but it could have been a million and one other places. It might have been a dark cellar in Albania or a garage in Poland, a lavish cathedral in San Francisco or a makeshift portacabin in the Australian outback, a country church in Buckinghamshire or a converted warehouse in Brixton. In fact, it is a conventional, nineteenth-century church building somewhere in inner London. It is Sunday morning and people are gathering for a celebration of the Christian Eucharist. In those million and one other places the group would have varied culturally and socially, but the inner voices would be some of the heart rumours of humanity. This book ends by listening to some of those inner voices as they wait to worship God.

Joan sits quietly giggling in the middle of a group from the local home for the mentally handicapped:

> God mistook me. Jesus mistake.
> Sleep on now, I must come to you.
> Lord of Lights, flees from you I do,
> I shall not want or wish to take.
> Me mistake. God mistake.
> Here I shall be born from a father.
> In my land of bliss, a snake ate
> the rose. God mistake.
> I shall be born under the rose bush.
> If God doesn't make a mistake.

Michael walks in with his wife and two small children. He looks jaded, having flown back from Kenya the day before. He was meeting executives in part of the multi-national corporation for which he works:

MICHAEL 'WHITE':   It's exhausting me, all this flying round the world . . . I feel dead deep inside.

MICHAEL 'BLACK':   It's all hopeless. Curl up and die.

MICHAEL 'WHITE':   Oh, that old seductive voice again . . . telling me there's no hope left. All that murmuring about death.

MICHAEL 'BLACK':   There's no meaning or value in it all. It's all in vain. Carry on with your business . . . that's what you call it, don't you? Pull the plug on all this.

MICHAEL 'WHITE':   The Kingdom of God . . . what's all this about? Transforming the face of the earth? Well, that's what we're trying to do in Kenya . . . oh God, have we got it right . . .?

MICHAEL 'BLACK':   Give it up . . . the fields are full of deadly poppies. Enjoy yourself . . . you don't need to agonise like this. Your bed is covered with roses.

MICHAEL 'WHITE':   It's wilderness out there . . . but I saw for true. I can't go on like this . . . how can I struggle with the Christ who struggles in that compromised world . . . I'm torn, broken, fragmented. God, I'm exhausted.

MICHAEL 'BLACK':   There is no meaning; it's all hopeless, all vain, there's no way through. You'll never get this lot together.

MICHAEL 'WHITE':   I remember the face of that poor black man . . . He didn't say much but one thing I remember, 'You must always struggle for the light'.

MICHAEL 'BLACK':   Ha! Ha! Ha!

MICHAEL 'WHITE':   I'm living close to the abyss . . . but that's why I'm here. Remember that day I came back six years ago? He still loves me.

Susan is a young mother with three children. Her husband refuses to come anywhere near a church but says it's OK for Susan to do her thing. She's left two children in the Sunday school and one in the creche:

Phew . . . just made it again. Don't feel particularly religious . . . still I never do. Funny that. I always just make it but I never feel like I think I should. I just don't have great feelings . . . Suppose the vicar must have . . . still, I belong here and I come because I have to. Can't help it. I just can't understand why Kevin doesn't feel any need for it. Says he can get on quite well enough without a daddy in the sky . . . odd, 'cos his dad left him when he was three. God, why doesn't that Mary leave her kid in the creche . . . I want a bit of peace. Well, I'm here and that's what matters. Kevin, it does make a difference . . . especially to me as a woman.

Daniel is preparing the censer in the vestry. He's finding it hard to get the charcoal burning. He's West Indian and left school eighteen months ago. He's still unemployed. As he prepares, he hums:

Oh, by and by, by and by,
I'm gonna lay down my heavy load.

I know my robe's going to fit me well,
I've tried it on at the gates of hell.

O, hell is deep and a dark despair
O, stop, poor sinner, and don't go there!

O, by and by, by and by,
I'm gonna lay down my heavy load.

and he thinks: 'Will the dark brother always be the one to be shot?' and he hums:

Nobody knows the trouble I seen, Lord,
Nobody knows but Jesus.

Sylvia has recently retired from being a clerk at the local office of the DHSS. She has worshipped here since she was a child, except for five years when she transferred her affections to the local Methodist Church. She was married but now lives alone:

. . . felt funny for the last three weeks God that Bob doesn't look well at all hope I don't go like him only retired six months said he was really looking forward to it looks so ill

not sure where I'm going hope I don't get ill poor Ruby
not well at all her mum died a month ago said Ruby would
always be poorly had meningitis when she was 4 doctor
said she'd never be right again well he was right wore pink
taffeta at my wedding, poor thing, bridesmaid she was
never said anything 'All right' 'Yes' 'No' 'OK' we was out
shopping but all she'd say was 'All right' then she got
depressed perhaps she could come and live near me lives
in Charlton now I could look after her went to see her the
other day suppose you want a cup of tea she said I'm going
for my dinner now you can come but they won't give you
one her mum always kept open house everybody in the
street went in had a lovely lunch fish and potatoes and
peas and jam pudding and custard and tea only 40p the
council will have to move her she can't stay in sheltered
accommodation poor Ruby they're still treating her at the
hospital yes I could look after her perhaps that's what I'm
meant to be doing now what do you think Lord?

Jim is fifteen and lives about 300 yards from the church.
As he rolls over in bed to the faint sounds of Boy George on
Radio 1, he hears the clang of the church bell:

Oh God, that bloody racket again. Thank God, they don't
make me go there anymore. So bored and all this God
business. A lot of myths, that's what it is. He's a funny
bloke on the radio ... almost as funny as God. Bloke in
woman's clothes ... oh, God, just like the vicar!! (*Smiles to
himself.*) Don't know what I went along with that confirmation stuff for. It seemed right at the time but then what?
Nothing, absolutely nothing. The youth club's finished ...
anyway what the hell. We'll all be blown up by 1990.
Thank God I live in central London ... we'll be the first
to go. Won't know anything about it. God, I'm afraid ...
oh shut up, you're a man now. Funny bloke, funny music,
funny God ... I feel just like that telly advert. What did
she say he'd got? Torpor? Yes, that's me. I've got religious
torpor, too.

Peter is a senior civil servant in the Ministry of Defence.
He was divorced ten years ago but the vicar agreed to marry
him in church. Since the marriage both he and his wife have

been regular members of the congregation. He is a deputy churchwarden:

PETER: Wish I could have slept better last night.

VOICE: Well, why couldn't you? Something bugging you?

PETER: Not that I know of . . . well, suppose there must be . . . perhaps it's my age.

VOICE: Well, when do I get a chance to talk to you?

PETER: What do you mean? Don't you do it at a reasonable time?

VOICE: You're never around then. You're busy or you're working at home or answering phone calls from Bonn or Paris or Washington. Or you're rushing off to the opera . . . usually Wagner, isn't it?

PETER: What are you going on about?

VOICE: I want to talk to you about death and destruction and love.

PETER: Oh, I see . . . well, we have to defend this country. All this unilateral talk is sheer nonsense. Those Greenham Common women are a real menace . . . especially when they go in for all that pseudo-religious ritual.

VOICE: But I have already conquered death and destruction and violence and they are not going to have the final word.

PETER: Yes, well, I know all that and I sort of believe it but if we leave ourselves defenceless the Russians will slaughter us. And somewhere I've got a sneaking suspicion inside that we're all valueless anyway. We deserve to be destroyed.

VOICE: Peter, you don't understand very much about me, do you? You're so caught up in your talk and your illusions, you'll have forgotten this conversation by 10 a.m. tomorrow morning. I've conquered death. You don't have to be afraid and my nature is Love. 2 a.m. is the only time I can break through and let you know that.

PETER: What do you want me to do?

VOICE: Do? Peter, be astonished by hope.

The organ began to play. The crucifer appeared at the vestry door. The heart rumours of humanity quietened down. A stillness fell on the congregation.

And God listened.

Select Bibliography

Campbell, J., *Myths to Live by*, Souvenir Press.

Cirlot, J. E., *A Dictionary of Symbols*. Routledge.

Cuming, G., *The Godly Order*, Alcuin Club.

Davies, J. G., *Every Day God*, SCM Press.

Dix, Dom G., *The Shape of the Liturgy*. A & C Black.

Eliade, M., *The Myth of the Eternal Return*. Princeton University Press.

Jung, C. G., *The Collected Works* (especially vols. 9 & 11), Routledge.

Killinger, J., *Leave it to the Spirit: A Handbook for Experimental Worship*. SCM Press.

Lessa, W. and Vogt, E. *Reader in Comparative Religion*. Harper and Row.

Maitland, S., *A Map of the New Country*. Routledge.

Marshall, M., *Renewal in Worship*. Marshall, Morgan and Scott.

Michael, C. and Norrisey, M., *Prayer and Temperament*. The Open Door (USA).

Nelson, J. B., *Embodiment*. SPCK.

Perham, M., *Liturgy Pastoral and Parochial*. SPCK.

Perry, M., *The Paradox of Worship*. SPCK.

Schmemann, A., *Introduction to Liturgical Theology*. Faith Press.

Underhill, E., *Worship*. Longmans.

Watkins, K., *Faithful and Fair*. Abingdon (USA).

Weil, L., *Sacraments and Liturgy*. Blackwell.

Willimon, W., *Worship as Pastoral Care*. Abingdon (USA).

Index